ANTI-JEWISH PREJUDICES
IN GERMAN-CATHOLIC SERMONS

ANTI-JEWISH PREJUDICES
IN GERMAN-CATHOLIC SERMONS

Walter Zwi Bacharach

Translated from the Hebrew by

Chaya Galai

The Edwin Mellen Press
Lewiston/Queenston/Lampeter

Library of Congress Cataloging-in-Publication Data

Bachrach, Zvi.
    [Min ha-tselav el tselav ha-ķeres. English]
    Anti-Jewish prejudices in German-Catholic sermons / Walter Zwi
Bacharach ; translated from the Hebrew by Chaya Galai.
        p.   cm.
    Includes bibliographical references.
    ISBN 0-7734-9181-3
    1. Judaism--Controversial literature--History and criticism.
2. Antisemitism--Germany--History--19th century. 3. Christianity
and antisemitism. 4. Catholic Church--Germany--History-19th
century. 5. Germany--Ethnic relations. I. Title.
BM585.B2313 1993
261.2'6'094309034--dc20   92-37137
                                                           CIP

Originally published by Sifriat Poalim Ltd, Tel Aviv, Israel, 1991

A CIP catalog record for this book
is available from the British Library.

The Edwin Mellen Press   The Edwin Mellen Press
        Box 450   Box 67
Lewiston, New York   Queenston, Ontario
     USA 14092   CANADA L0S 1L0

                    Edwin Mellen Press, Ltd.
                    Lampeter, Dyfed, Wales
                    UNITED KINGDOM SA48 7DY

            Printed in the United States of America

For Hannah

TABLE OF CONTENTS

FOREWORD

I was encouraged to undertake this study by my friend, Professor Jacob Katz.

It was during the preliminary stages, when I was beginning to locate and collate material, that I found the primary sources, namely the priests' sermons, in the Library of Congress, Washington. There I was greatly helped by the staff, and particularly Mr. Bruce Martin, who spared no effort to assist me. In Germany I found important documents in the Municipal Library of Moenchengladbach, which has a rich collection of Catholic documents. This includes the archival collection of the Volksverein fuer das Katholische Deutschland. The Library Director, Dr. Manfred Wermter and his staff placed all the required documents at my disposal. I examined nineteenth century Catholic periodicals in the Bavarian National Library. Diverse additional material was made available to me by the National Library of West Berlin, and reached me through the generous assistance of Dr. Regina Melka and Ms. Monika Martini. The illuminating comments of my friend, Professor Werner Jochmann, former Director of the Hamburg Institute for the Study of National Socialism, contributed greatly to my understanding of the annals of German Catholics.

To all these people and institutions, I would like to express my heartfelt thanks. Without their help and support, I could not have completed their task. To my wife, Hannah, I owe the greatest debt. With great forbearance, she tolerated a husband who was deeply involved in depressing and disturbing literature. I dedicate this work to her.

The Author

CHAPTER ONE

PERSONAL QUESTIONS

I wrote the following study, which deals with the attitudes of non-Jew towards Jews, as a researcher in the field of contemporary history. My previous research was devoted to Nazi ideology. The subject which now engages me is the attitude of Catholics towards Jews in nineteenth century Germany. The reader may well ask whether the order in which I have chosen to study these subjects is not anachronistic? Does not historical logic require the scholar to proceed from the nineteenth century to the twentieth? From the viewpoint of scientific discipline, this claim is indeed valid. But, at the same time, there are two factors entailed in any scientific study: the first is the theme, and the second is the personality of the researcher. I feel, therefore, that it is relevant to start out by mentioning my own personal involvement in the subjects with which I have been dealing for some years.

I am a Holocaust survivor. At the age of eighteen, I arrived in Israel in order to rebuild my life. As I reached adulthood, during my years at university, I felt the impact of the traumatic experiences I had undergone. Among my outstanding teachers were the late Professors Jacob Talmon and Uriel Tal. Perhaps unknowingly, they heightened my awareness of my past. I am not referring to consciousness of my Jewish identity or identification with Zionist ideology. My studies brought to the surface certain painful, penetrating questions which had troubled me since the Holocaust. When Professor Talmon wrote that "the discarding of awe and reverence, the disappearance of the restraints which prevent deviant acts - these do not occur overnight; this is a gradual and protracted process of "dialectical development."[1] I immediately asked myself what had caused the deviation in the course of German history which had caused us so much suffering? What was the nature of that protracted process which had dragged millions, and me among them, into a world permeated with bottomless hatred of Jews? My curiosity was born out of stunned horror, it sought the answer to my own personal existence, which I perceived as a kind of rebirth. I was increasingly preoccupied with these questions, since I grasped that there must be historical explanations for all those terrible events, that the Holocaust was perpetrated by human beings, it was devised and executed by ordinary, normal mortals. I knew then and know still that I am a man like other men, with frailties and good qualities - and this knowledge requires no substantiation. I know from my own bitter experience that in that inferno, all of us were human beings, all - both murderers and victims. It was this knowledge, acquired at first hand, which has haunted me ever since. Chief Justice Chaim Cohen has said, referring to the Holocaust "Since the birth of Christianity, if not before, history has not touched us directly. We knew, of course, about the persecutions and about those Jews 'led like lambs to the slaughter'. We knew, but did not sense directly. But when you suddenly feel the sensation on your own flesh, when you see the bloodshed with your own eyes, everything takes on a new meaning."[2] I had studied the history of Nazism, history which "touched us directly" - as a nation, and affected me as an inflicted such suffering on us, on my immediate family, my relatives and my friends, and on me. The older I grew, the greater was my need to understand.

I found the psychoanalytical answer to my questions to be unsatisfactory, leaving the larger questions unsolved. It has already been said that "analytical theory has proved incapable of tackling the body of historical facts, and has not found its place among the research methods which attempt to investigate them."[3]

It is a historical fact that I, together with tens of thousands of others, was incarcerated in that hell on earth because I am a Jew, and that my only sin was that I had been born a Jew.

One day in the camp, a certain guard approached me during a parade and asked me if I knew why I was there. When I remained silent, he slaps my face and shouted: "Weil du ein Jude bist!" ("Because you are a Jew"). As adult, I wanted to understand what motivated that Nazi, what had nurtured his ideology, how he perceived Jews, how human-beings could act in this fashion. These questions underlaid my research on Nazi racism. But the same research impelled me to query further. Can the mere fact of our being Jews explain how the mass murders were planned and perpetrated in cold blood in so short a period - to be exact, between 1941-1945? Is it really possible to rouse an entire nation to awareness and conviction of the need to commit genocide within a period of four to five years? It is inconceivable that in so brief a span, masses of people could have been persuaded to exterminate the Jews, to obliterate their memory from the face of the earth. In the camps I witnessed the profound revulsion, the contempt, the hatred, the brutality demonstrated towards us as Jews, and not only on the part of the Nazis. Those who shared my fate, the Russian prisoners of war, the non-Jewish Polish political prisoners, although we suffered together - despised me for my Jewishness. All these queries stimulated my desire to know more, and led me from conclusion to cause, or, in the language of history - from the Holocaust itself back to the annals of traditional anti-semitism. My study of Nazi ideology shifted the focus of my interest to one of the main sources of anti-semitism, Christian Catholic hatred of Jews.

In the search after the roots of that hatred, I confronted a question which many had asked before me. How can there be a connection between the anti-Christian Nazi anti Semitism and Christian hatred of Jews? Or, in other words - how could a true Christian identify with the Nazi outlook? It is, however, a fact that Hitler, who perpetrated the Holocaust, was a Catholic who never officially abandoned the church. What is even more surprising is that the church never excommunicated him nor banished him from its ranks. Hitler attacked Christianity only after he had discovered that the Church was unwilling to accept his racial theories. In 1934 he expressed his views to the evangelical bishops Wurm[*] and Meiser,[*] and demanded that the church adopt the new doctrine of blood and race. If the Church refused, he declared, "historical development will pass it over".[4] This indicates that, at

4

the outset, he tried to implement his anti-Jewish policy as a Christian, and did not reject Christianity outright on Principle. He approved of Jesus "a man who, as a single individual with only a handful of supporters, recognized who the Jews were and called for a struggle against them...and he died bleeding on the cross." In Christ he saw "a popular leader (Volksfuehrer) who stood up to Judaism."[5] It was only when it became clear to him that the Church rejected the new doctrine, that he attacked it as synonymous with Judaism and with Bolshevism. But whereas he was uncompromisingly opposed to Judaism and Bolshevism, his approach to the Church and to Christianity was tactical. In 1941 he declared that it was possible to shatter the power of the Church all at once, and that that it should be left to its own devices, to dwindle and disappear in due course.[6] His attitude towards the Church remained ambivalent and though he rejected its tenets of faith, he was ready to learn from its methods, organization and standpoint vis a vis the Jews. And, in fact, Hitler collected all the popular anti-Jewish diatribes. It was from this collection that I studied the Catholic anti-Jewish views disseminated in Germany.

I am well aware of the grave implications of the claim that there was a connection between Catholic doctrine and the crimes of Hitler. However the analogy is inevitable because of the similarity between their anti-Jewish arguments. In historical research one cannot, of course, speak of identity; the historian is interested in similarities. And, moreover, if Hitler did in fact draw his terrible conclusions from these diatribes, it is our obligation to study their historical background.

The terms Christianity, church, Catholicism, Christian doctrine are used here interchangeably. This method invites criticism on grounds of generalization. Yet, I believe that, in discussing the Christian outlook on the Jews, we may assume the existence of a consensus. The two camps, Protestant and Catholic, did not differ greatly in their dissemination of the negative image of the Jew. A study of lower middle class and evangelist rural public opinion in Germany before the rise of Nazism, referred in its conclusions to "the distortion of Judaism imprinted on the minds of the readers of the Sunday press".

It should not be assumed, of course, that this focus in Catholicism stems from the fact that Hitler was a Catholic. Long before the appearance of Protestantism in the 16th century, it was Catholicism which shaped the stereotyped image of the Jew, and this image influenced the course of history. A number of important studies have already been written on Protestantism.[7a]

I have sought to examine the nature of the information about the Jew transmitted by Catholic preachers in their sermons in church, and its presentation in the handbooks they consulted, in order to see whether Judaism was distorted by Catholicism as well. The material I cite relates generally to information conveyed to rural and lower middle class populations in cities and towns in various parts of Germany.

The findings of this study speak for themselves. Historically speaking I now understand the source of the denial of Judaism and of the contempt for Jews. It is undoubtedly possible to combine together all the anti-Jewish elements in the Christian outlook and to obtain an image, which casts light on the meaning of the hostility and the anti-semitism. Apart from historical curiosity in itself, which demands responsible exposure of the true facts, it is to be hoped that the present study will, even if only obliquely, rouse those Christian elements who have slandered and degraded the Jews for centuries, to ponder and to realize how great is the responsibility resting on them. Perhaps they may then join those, both Protestant and Catholic who are now seeking ways of making amends.

When I return, in thought, to the death camp at Birkenau, I find that I now understand better whence grew the denial of my Judaism. But the horrors of Auschwitz-Birkenau are still beyond my understanding.

NOTES

[*] For names marked with asterisk, see appendix with biographical details.

1.   Talmon, *be-Idan ha-Alimut*, p. 267. (Hebrew)

2.   Cohen, *Shofet Elyon*, p. 127. (Hebrew)

3.   Katz, Sinat Yisrael, p. 224. (Hebrew)

4.   Scholder, in Kulka, p. 189.

5.   Jäckel, *Aufzeichnungen*, p. 623, Jochmann, Monologe, p. 91.

6.   *Ibid.*, p. 83, 150.

7.   Arndt, *Die Judenfrage*, p. 221.

In 1981 a dissertation was published entitled "The Jews and the Death of Christ: Anti-Jewish motifs in Protestant religious works for elementary schools." The conclusions state, inter alia: "Analysis showed that most a these works still contain anti-Jewish statements....despite several positive beginnings, there is still a generally negative approach, which relates to the Jews with contempt." (p. 212). In the foreword, the author writes: "After completion of the manuscript, a parallel study was published by Peter Fiedler of Freiburg University, entitled 'Judaism in the teachings of the Catholic religion'. His conclusions are strikingly identical to my own. It is challenging ecumenical mission to renew relations between Christians an Jews." Olmesdahl

7a.   Oberman; Tal.

CHAPTER TWO

THE THEOLOGICAL-CHRISTIAN NEED

Any study dealing with the history of the Jews within a non- Jewish society, confronts the problem of determining the reason why they were hated as a minority. One such study opens with the statement: "No human being is born with hatred in his blood. He is usually infected with hatred through contact."[1] Social contact between Jews and non-Jews existed in various spheres and in different forms, and was usually hostile rather than friendly. This fact in itself raises the question of the source of this enmity. Is there, in the annals of this confrontation between the Jews and the world around them, some constant irritant? Was the historical hostility one-sided or can the complexity of the relations be explained as resulting from some mutual repulsion? It is permissible to conclude today, on the basis of a large body of research, that since the Middle Ages there has been some constant factor generating negative tension between the Jews and their surroundings. It stems from the encounter between the two monotheistic religions, Christianity and Judaism. All the disputes between Jews and non-Jews - excluding the encounter between Islam and Judaism, were based on religious antagonism. It has been truly said that "the unique continuity which endured through thousands of years of oppression of the Jews....is evident in the fact that the overwhelming majority of Europeans were Christians heart and soul."[2] Even the anti-Christian Nazi outlook drew inspiration from the totally negative image attributed by Christian theology to the Jews.[3] We can

8

now focus the question of the onesidedness or reciprocity of the historical enmity between Christianity and Judaism. Some historians have favoured the 'one-sided' theory. One of the Catholics among them surveyed in detail the history of Jewish suffering, concluding that the attitude of disrespect of the synagogue towards the young Christian church, its consistently hostile attitude towards those Jews who converted to Christianity, its active efforts to recruit support among Christians - all these roused the Church Fathers to perceive the Jews as a threat to the Christian religion.[4] In fact, the Jewish response to Christian dogma was profound aversion. However, to refuse to acknowledge the anti-Jewish element inherent from the outset in Christian theology, is to deny a historical truth. "Revulsion from Jewish life, which was essentially theological, and later became emotional as well, is one of the cornerstones of Christian anti-Jewish feeling, which is an important component of anti-semitism."[5] And, indeed, the accusation levelled at the Jews, namely that they had murdered Christ, is an amendment of the real charge against them, namely, that they had refused to adopt Christianity. It was this refusal, according to the Christian view, which condemned them to eternal exile, or, in cruder form, was considered a Divine punishment for the crucifixion of the Messiah."[6] Thus, Flusser perceived the history of the Christian-Jewish conflict as a theological conflict, which eventually took on emotional dimensions. If the dispute had continued to be a theological dialogue, the history of the Jews might have taken a very different direction. However, sober and disinterested clarification of issues in dispute was replaced by increasingly emotional debate, by denunciations and accusations, culminating in fierce hatred. Christianity, which had regarded itself as the legal and historical heir to Judaism and claimed the birthright, no longer considered Judaism to be a worthy partner in theological debate, but rather as a religion which had forfeited its right to exist. And since it refused to accept the Christian verdict, and adamantly insisted on preserving its unique heritage and tradition, then its only function was "to serve as testimony, trial and symbol."[7] Because of their intransigeance, the Jews were destined to bear witness to the triumph of the Christian religion Judaism was not judged by its content, sacred or secular 'others', that is to say Christian theologians, determined the image of the Jew according to what they wished to consider as Jewish."[8]   By determining the lowly and debased status of the Jews, Christianity segregated them and discriminated against them.

The theologian, like the philosopher, constantly ponders the larger questions concerning the essence of divinity and of the relations between God and man. The ideologist is concerned with answers, not questions. He has a stock of ready answers to historical conditions and phenomena, through which he seeks to establish facts congenial to him and compatible with his interests. In the confrontation between Christianity and Judaism, theology was transformed into ideology.

Religions, and Christianity among them, have overt objectives. They aspire to influence their believers and supporters through sacred books whose dictates and precepts determine the relations between man and his God. But in addition to the overt aims, there are also covert aspirations. These are at odds with the open message of revelationary religion, and are in fact a distortion of that message. An authority on Christian theology has denoted these aims 'ideological',[9] since they are a response to the social needs of a specific period, and because they are of transient nature, and have nothing to do with the eternal and divine truth. At the same time, these ideologies were so intricately entwined with the religious message, and had left so deep an imprint on human consciousness, that it is difficult to discern the dividing line between religious truth and ideological distortion.

In light of the catastrophic events of the twentieth century, it is no longer possible to ignore those ideological elements which distorted the content of the scriptures. After the fall of the Nazi regime, certain scholars, both Jewish and Christian, pointed an accusing finger at Christianity. "The responsibility of the Germans for these crimes is secondary, and attached itself, like some loathsome parasite, to an ancient tradition, namely the Christian tradition."[10]

The connection between Christian theology and Christian hatred of Jews has been noted by many authorities, from various viewpoints. The points of dispute between the two religions have been analysed and dissected in detail and to list them here would be an awesome task.

The twentieth century is the century of the Holocaust of the Jews, which can be perceived as the culmination of the catastrophe of traditional hatred of Jews. The mass extermination was carried out from Nazi motives and through Nazi planning. Nazism is one of the manifestations of the German historical tradition. The planning and implementation of the Holocaust, in all its appalling scope, have been the subject of separate historical research.[11] In contrast, the history of the hatred, the annals of anti-semitism in the decades preceding the Holocaust, have been described as an issue in its own right.[12] And, in fact, the history of the relations between Jews and non-Jews in the nineteenth and twentieth centuries differs from that of earlier centuries. One might say that the relations were now increasingly dynamic rather than static as the Jews emerged from their involuntary isolation and were integrated into non-Jewish society, and were perceived as rivals and competitors. Their emancipation revived age-old anti-Jewish slogans, and lent them a new dimension, in the form of overt conflict between the Gentile granting emancipation and the tolerated Jew.[13]

The following pages deal with the history of those anti-Jewish Catholic slogans in pre-Holocaust German society.

The two main sources for the dissemination of anti-Jewish propaganda are interconnected. The first is contained in Christian dogma and the in views of the church fathers and of the official church theologians.[14] Their dogmatic outlook determined attitudes towards the Jews and served as a guideline for the Catholic catechism. The statements of the church fathers were of supreme importance in creating the image of the Jew for generations to come. These views were formulated in the second to fifth centuries, as research has shown. By then, the Jew had already forfeited " his real, flesh and blood image and become a vague one-dimensional, negative and satanic figure, fashioned out of a mosaic of negative verses and statements, in the Old and New Testaments. This image, therefore, was based not on the true situation and conduct of the Jews, but on the stereotype created by Christian theology....and thus it happened that, because of the authority of the authors and their subsequent prestige, exercises in interpretation and statements inspired by untrammeled hostility, taken in conjunction with the New Testament, influenced the Christian attitude towards the Jewish people in the Middle Ages and in modern times..."[15]

It was the "Christian theological need" which created the distorted image of the Jew for generations to come. The dispute between Jews and Christians over theological questions, should have been conducted on the theoretical factual plane. And this has in fact been and is so today as well, under the shadow of the Holocaust. However, in order to understand the processes which led up to that catastrophe, the scholar must turn to the second source for explanation of the consolidation of hatred of Jews.

This source is connected, not to ideology and theology, but to the social sphere, and is related to the continuous contact between Christians from the lower classes, and Jews. Facts were determined not by the abstract image shaped by the theological commentaries of the Church Fathers and the authors of various dogmas, but by the real presence of the Jews, as perceived by the Christian masses. The concrete image born out of the everyday contacts, was a negative one. The common people had no interest in theological theories, and adopted the readymade negative image, seeking therein the blame for their own misfortunes, failures and omissions. For the common people, the Jew symbolized the dark mythical forces which threatened the social order. The unlearned individual does not grasp the subtleties of 'scientific anti-semitism' and is not aware of theological hatred of Jews, but easily grasps the practical implications.[16] They open his eyes to the possibility of transferring the blame for all his troubles onto the Jew and his accursed actions of long ago. The common people were remote from the theologians and philosophers in their ivory towers, who painted a negative picture of the Jews in scholarly, high-flown language, based on the scriptures. But if not the theologians, then who instructed the peasants, the villagers, the labourers? Where did the German masses learn their hatred of the Jews?

The sources influencing the untutored masses had to be suitably popular and simple in content. One of the important sources from which they drew their stereotypical view of the Jews was the popular literature disseminated in Germany in the nineteenth century. George Mosse has pointed out the importance of this type of literature for understanding of the adoption of anti-Jewish views by the German public. He has analysed the popular views, trivial in themselves, which were reflected in this literature.[17] The impact of this literature was dependent on the ability and readiness of the masses to read it. But, as is always the case, many of the common people were semi-illiterate and found reading difficult. The written word demands a certain intellectual effort, leisure time and willingness. A simpler, and perhaps more effective method is the oral transmission of messages. In this fashion, the content can be deliberately adapted to the mentality and understanding of the audience. A preacher can direct his remarks so as to stir the emotions of his audience. Through their sermons, popular preachers were able to revive that "emotional revulsion from Judaism" mentioned above. There was no more popular preacher than the ecclesiastical preacher. In villages and towns, the faithful flocked, (as they still do today), to hear his Sunday sermons in church, and absorb his message. Friedrich Nietzsche was well aware of the persuasive power of the sermon, and wrote: But in Germany....there was but one type of public and artistic address: that delivered from the pulpit. Only the preacher from the pulpit has known till now the weight of the syllable, of the word, the power of a sentence to thrust, to bend, to break through, to speed to conclusion."[18]

Popular literature, reinforced by popular sermons, on the one hand, intellectual theories and the conduct of politicians, on the other - combined to shape public opinion on the Jews in nineteenth century Germany. Nietzsche wrote in this context, "Hearken: I have yet to meet a German who felt any fondness for the Jews."[19]

NOTES

1.   Malcolm Hay, p. 9.

2.   Gottfried Schramm, p. 318.

3.   Katz, From Prejudice to Destruction, Anti-Semitism, 1700-1933, Cambridge, Ma. 1980,: "Anti-Semites wished to perpetuate the inferior position of Jews, or even reinstitute some features of their pre-emancipatory situation. Thus, even if they negated the Christian motives responsible for the creation of the situation, anti-Semites still took it as the basis of their operation. There is a patent historical continuity between the two phases of the Jewish predicament," Katz quotes Jules Isaac who implied "that Christianity is accountable for all the enormities of modern anti-Semitism, including its culmination in the Holocaust." (321). He claims that "the historian, once he becomes involved in the question of responsibility (like Isaac Z.B.) must pay attention to what may seem to contradict his judgment. According to Katz, it was "the Christian apologists, as well as anti-Semitic ideologists, who acquitted Christianity of the charge of having gostered anti-Semitism," because, as they claimed, "anti-Jewish sentiments and even atrocities" existed in the ancient world. (321/2). Interestingly, Katz admits that "astonishingly enough, Isaac succeeded in attracting into his orbit theologians and believing Christians." (321).

4.   Flannery, p. 276.

5.   Flusser, Judaism...p. 451.

6.   *Ibid*, p. 449; see also Katz, Ghetto, p. 15.

      On the ideology, see Flusser, *ibid*., p. 360: "Every ideology is based on theoretical interweaving and objectivization of a basic emotional attitude existing between the speaker and his object." In Flusser's polemics with modern theologians who seek to prove the existence of a conflict between the message of Christ and the ideology of the Jews of his time, he defines their tendentious method "as an subject for study in the research on ideology', which has no room in modern New Testament research. According to Flusser, all the sources attest to the fact "that Jesus said not one word which could have seriously affronted any Jew." See also Bacharach, Ideologies, p. 7-11.

7.   Talmon, p. 279.

8.   Parkes, "The Jew became what circumstances made him...It was Christendom which decided that the price of that loyalty should be psychological and social degradation."

14

9.   Klein, p. 7.

10.   Isaac, p. 167.   Hebrew translation in Hay, p. 15.   And see also quotations from studies by Parkes and Pierre van Passen.

11.   See Yahil and Hilberg.

12.   Several works in Hebrew should be noted: Katz, Sinat Yisrael (Anti-semitism), Ettinger, Almog, Bacharach.

13.   Katz, Jakob, "Christian Jewish Antagonism on the eve of the modern era. In Kulka, p. 34.

14.   Kenneth Stowe. "Hatred of Jews or love of the church: the papal approach to the Jews" (Hebrew). In Almog, Sinat Yisrael, pp. 91-113.

15.   *Ibid.*, p. 87.

16.   Trachtenberg, p. 4.

17.   Mosse, Germans and Jews, p. 62; Mosse, Crisis.

18.   Nietzsche, Beyond Good and Evil, § 247.

19.   *Ibid.*, § 251.

CHAPTER THREE

THE STANDING OF THE CATHOLICS IN GERMANY AFTER THE FRENCH REVOLUTION - HISTORICAL BACKGROUND

This survey of relations between Jews and Catholics in Germany, focuses mainly on the period from the second half of the nineteenth century to the First World War. There are several reasons why these time limits have been set. Firstly, I felt it important to emphasize the historical continuity between the modern period, characterized by the upsurge of anti-semitism and culminating in the Holocaust, and the earlier era. The period between the two world wars has already been the subject of study,[1] but this fact in itself is not sufficient justification for excluding it from the present survey. A weightier consideration was the fact that German Catholicism has constituted an integral part of modern German history, so that the 1848-1918 period is as significant for the annals of Catholicism as it is for Germany as a whole.

These seven decades were marked by the social emancipation of the Germans from traditional frameworks.[2] In passing, it is worth noting two developments, influenced by the French Revolution, which left a deep imprint on German history in general and German Catholicism in particular. The first of these was the confiscation of church lands by the state, namely the secularization of church property, which is relevant to our discussion because of its impact on attitudes towards the Jews.

The Catholic church in Germany suffered a heavy blow at the beginning of the nineteenth century. The conquest of the Rhineland by

Napoleon's armies had far-reaching consequences for the country, and weakened the church at the same time. German Catholicism suffered a similar fate to the French church. In the prevailing revolutionary and anti-ecclesiastical atmosphere, church lands were confiscated in the occupied areas of the Rhineland. In 1803 the Reichsdeputationshauptschluss decided on the secularization of church lands on the right bank of the Rhine, as compensation for French confiscation of the lands of German princes on the left bank, according to the Luneville treaty. This measure undermined the power which the church derived from its vast property-holdings. In 1815, the Vienna Congress restored the left bank of the Rhine to Germany, but not the church lands.[3]

The attrition of ecclesiastical independence had enduring consequences for German Catholicism. Volens nolens, the future of the church was now bound up with a secular authority, with which it was obliged to maintain constant contact in order to promote and preserve its interests. The Catholic camp in Germany underwent politicization as a result. At the same time, there was growing support for Ultramontanism, i.e. rapprochement with the Vatican. Thus, secularization and religious extremism evolved concomitantly.

The extremist trend found expression in the *Literarischer Verein zur Aufrechterhaltung Verteidigung und Auslegung der Roemischkatholischen Religion* (Literary Association for the Maintenance, Protection and Interpretation of the Roman-Catholic Religion). Based in Bavaria, it consisted of 50 representatives of the German bishoprics, and its proclaimed aim was to promote the practical demands of the church.[4] In addition to the Ultramontanists, a 'romantic' group of philosophers and scholars was founded, among whose prominent members were Josef Goerres[*] and Adam Mueller[*]. Up to 1837, this group was characterized by ideological opposition to the ideals of the Enlightenment, liberalism and rationalism. Later, it shared a common language with political romanticism. These trends glorified the German past, and fostered such concepts as the 'organic state' and 'organic nationalism'. According to this latter concept, the German people was an entity born out of immanent and organic, rather than voluntary-mechanical forces.[5] (From the eighteen thirties onward, this movement played a decisive part in the development of German nationalism. However, this subject is outside the scope of the present study.)

An affair which occurred in Cologne in 1837 had considerable impact on the consolidation of Catholic forces. Two years previously, the Bishop of Muenster, Clemens August, Freiherr Droste zu Vischering had been appointed Archbishop of Cologne. The Prussian authorities soon discovered that they had committed an error of judgment, since the Archbishop was soon revealed to be an uncompromising Catholic. A fierce struggle soon erupted around two issues. Firstly, a professor of theology named George Hermes had gathered around him a group of disciples with the aim of introducing intellectual elements into religious and theological thought, and enlisting pure reason in the cause of faith. The Prussian authorities viewed his activities with equanimity, but the Archbishop excommunicated him, forbidding students to attend his lectures. The second affair had graver implications, since it intensified the rivalries between Protestants and Catholics. The issue at point was mixed marriages between them. Prussian law stipulated that the sons of such marriages should be raised according to the religion of the father, and the daughters according to the mother's religion. The senior Protestant officials who were beginning to settle in areas with Catholic majorities, particularly Silesia, were particularly affected by this law. Since many of them married Catholic women, their daughters, by law, were raised as Catholics. Friedrich Wilhelm III issued a general edict in 1803, according to which all legitimate offspring of both sexes would be raised according to the father's religion. In 1815, Rhineland-Westphalia was annexed to Prussia, and in 1825 the edict was extended to these areas.

The Catholic clergy considered these measures to be manifestations of open hostility towards Catholicism, and Archbishop Droste refused to recognize them. In the 'Cologne incident' of 1837, the Archbishop was arrested by order of the authorities.[6] The outcry which followed on this arrest served at the pretext for a rallying of Catholic forces.

As this brief survey indicates, the Catholic camp was both weak and divided, on the defensive against the anti-religious forces which were gaining strength, inspired by the Enlightenment and the outcome of the French Revolution. This political feebleness and the onslaught on church assets in the first half of the nineteenth century, stimulated a strong desire for internal spiritual cohesion, as refuge from external pressures. Bishop Wilhelm Emmanuel von Ketteler[*] expressed this mood when he said that nowhere in this world was there an absolutely corrupt deed, even if it caused great damage. Everything was directed by the Divine will.[7]

If this were so, what benefit could Catholics derive from impoverishment, and what positive lesson could they learn from it? Catholic leaders and preachers sought to transform weakness into a source of renewed strength. Poverty and dispossession were depicted as the ideal. Jesus, through his deeds, had sanctified poverty, they argued, and hence every true believer must follow in the footsteps of his Lord. In this mood of spiritual revival, on the one hand, and social and economic decline, on the other, lies the connection to Judaism and the Jews, since the latter were depicted as the antithesis of the 'ideal of poverty'. Prosperity and wealth, the symbols of temporal power - that same power which was now slipping away from the Catholics - were identified with the image of the Jew. The precarious situation of Catholicism bolstered the traditional anti-Jewish emotions which had existed since the birth of Christianity. As the craving for religious and moral renewal grew in intensity, anti-Jewish attacks increased. The enemies of Catholicism were perceived as synonymous with the Jews, and in sermons, and in public opinion in general, Protestants were often described similarly to Jews. After 1837, anti-semitic action took on more organized form.

Catholic activity was focused in Mainz and Munich. The daily *Der Katholik* was founded in Mainz in 1821, as the voice of the struggle for independence of the German Catholic church. It played a decisive role in disseminating anti-Jewish propaganda. The above-mentioned 1837 'Cologne incident' led to the establishment in Munich of another influential paper, *Historische-Politische Blaetter*, the mouthpiece of Catholic conservatism in Germany, and the first real manifestation of political Catholicism. The editors, Goerres and Jarke, provided a conservative viewpoint of the everyday realities of political life, and attacked revolutionism, liberalism and modernism, denouncing them as anti-German and Jewish.[7a] In the context of attacks on Judaism, another trend should be noted, stemming directly from Catholic reorganizational efforts. A new 'social Catholicism' emerged, grounded on concern for the common good and the fostering of a spirit of Christian cooperation. Loyal to conservative ideals, this group called for the liberation of the workers from the stifling embrace of enslaving technology and capitalist exploitation. A new type of leader emerged for the masses, both rural populations and industrial workers - the social priest.[8] His mission was to instill in the workers, who had been exploited and debased by industrialization and modern trends, a sense of pride and self-esteem. The revival of religious faith was proposed as the remedy for social distress and degradation. The clarion call to the masses was accompanied by vitriolic attacks on the Jews, who were depicted as deniers of Christ and as the temporal representatives of the Devil.

The second phenomenon was expressed in the social changes which Germany was undergoing. The process of secularization was accompanied by the disintegration of the feudal-aristocratic structure, of which the church hierarchy had been part, and paved the way for the liberalization of these institutions. Those members of the clergy who held more enlightened social views, were now able to find their place more easily in the pervading liberal atmosphere.[8a]

The impact of these political and social changes on the church institutions reached its peak in the second half of the nineteenth century. This process offers an additional argument in favour of the relevance of this specific period for our study.

From the social and political viewpoints, German Catholicism took on organized form only after 1848. While representatives of the German people were seeking to arrive at a liberal consensus at the National Assembly in Frankfurt, the Catholics were trying to establish a cohesive framework at their first assembly in Mainz. In the same year, in Wuerzburg, the bishops established a center of their own. Matters reached such a pass that an attempt was made, on the initiative of Ignaz Doellinger,[9] to unify the leadership of German Catholicism under a separate German ecclesiastical constitution. This scheme was thwarted by the Vatican, which was wary of attempts to create foci of power outside its own sphere of control. This struggle for an independent German church authority, and the reaction of the Vatican, undoubtedly heightened the political awareness of German

Catholics. This awareness took concrete, organized form between 1848 and 1870, when Germany was on the road to unification.[10] The Catholic struggle against the Protestant Prussian government, the disputes within the Catholic camp itself, and the attempts to break free of Vatican domination - all these shaped attitudes towards the Jews.

Many books have been written about the relations between the Christian and Jewish religions, and between Christians and Jews - sometimes referred to as 'the Jewish question.' It is generally agreed that these relations are characterized by a theological dispute, which has been coloured by centuries of hostility towards the Jews. Some scholars see positive aspects in this religious tension, arguing that the struggle for the birthright and the disputes over Scriptural interpretations are indications of a sincere search for Divine truth. Both Christianity and Judaism aspire to acknowledgement of the existence of one sole God and, through this shared religious aspiration, they seek to encompass all mankind. Their paths may differ, it is claimed, but the final goal is the same. There is no reason for each to deny the validity of the other, since thereby, in effect, they are denying divinity itself.[11]

Theoretically speaking, this theological assumption is interesting and invites sober consideration. However, history has shown that this debate was never resolved at the negotiation table; the rivalry always spilled over to the everyday sphere. There, it was the simplistic and practical elements, the crude language of the masses of Christian believers, which predominated and reflected attitudes towards the Jews and Judaism. Religious tensions did not generate the fruitful encounter for which some philosophers had hoped.[12]

As noted above, the status of the Jews was discussed from church pulpits. Priests discussed the Jews, their beliefs, their writings and the role which Christ, the redeemer, had assigned to them. The statements were crude and dogmatic, and were presented as absolute truths, in clear and unambiguous language.[13] The priests considered it their mission to disseminate the church's message through their sermons. These men lived in rural surroundings or in small towns, and their sermons attest to their low intellectual level, and simple outlook, which was not inspired by abstract theological reasoning. The priests were involved in the everyday lives of their flock and adapted their sermons to their audience. At the same time, it should be emphasized that the new breed of rural social priest had absorbed few of the modern ideas. Far from the towns and cities, where the new rationalist philosophies were emerging, the priests called for a revival of faith, and this demand was at odds with the spirit of the times.[14]

The style of the sermons can be ascertained from one typical example. It deals allegorically with 'false wine' (Gefaelschter Wein), the wine being taken to symbolize faith. "What is false wine? You too may have heard the empty phrase: 'it does not matter what you believe, the important thing is to lead a decent life'. It does not matter to which religious community you belong; you may live a happy and honest life in any community. This attitude to faith and religion is known as 'indifferentismus', and it is this I call 'false wine'. For think how false is the statement: if you live a righteous life, you may believe in whatsoever you choose! Tell me, what would you reply to someone who came and declared that it matters not if you have legs or not, the important thing is to walk. You would answer curtly that he should stop uttering nonsense for how can one walk without legs? And, just as legs are vital for walking, so faith is essential for any life which is considered righteous in the eyes of God."[15] These simple words were accepted unquestionably by the audience, and were intended to raise the spirits of labourers and peasants struggling with threatening manifestations of modernism. What mattered to them was the spoken word of the priest and not the written Scriptures.

These references to the Jew were indelibly printed on the minds of naive Catholics when they encountered their Jewish neighbours. The Catholic catechism shaped the outlook of the preacher, and we shall examine its content below. There were also some Catholics, albeit few, who were aware that the picture of the Jew, as drawn in church sermons, was distorted.[16]

The language and style of the sermons were vivid and colourful. According to the introduction to one of the collections of homilies:[17] "Christian audiences will be more attentive to sermons, since through them, they reach the historical facts. In their imagination, they will feel themselves among the protagonists, will see their actions, hear their words, see with their own eyes the Lord Jesus, hear from his mouth his Divine teachings, and witness his miracles. These are spiritual visions which capture the listener entirely."[18] A sermon describing the Crucifixion illustrates vividly how to "capture the listener entirely." The brutal details were described in strong and sharp colours, which must have left their profound impact on the receptive audience. "And then his clothes, which had stuck to his reopened bleeding wounds of torture, were ripped off him, and thus his torn and still body was revealed to all....Now he was placed on the cross: arms and legs were fixed and bound by force, and nails, as thick as a finger, were hammered into the wood, through his hands and feet, through the fabric of nerves, veins and bones. The blood spouted wildly....Thus he hung stretched on the cross, with four open wounds, exposed to the light and the blazing sun of Palestine."[19]

This style does not appeal to the intellect. It plays on the emotions and can rouse the imagination of the masses, planting in their hearts the seed of hatred towards those who treated their Lord thus. And when such sermons were delivered in times of crisis and of anxieties, it is easy to understand how they roused the urge to seek an outlet for emotions at the expense of the Jew, who was the 'guilty party'.

NOTES

1.   Greive, *Theologie*.

2.   Alexander, in Moody, p. 441; Lill, in Rengstorf, p. 370; and see Thieme.

3.   Schnabel IV, p. 7ff; Bachem 1 pp. 33ff.

4.   Bergstrasser I, pp. 6ff.

5.   *Ibid.*, p. 6; Schnabel IV, pp. 164-172. The Catholics interpreted immanence as the Divine power which determined the mission of mankind, as individuals and as a whole. In this sense, the Divine order is seen as 'organic' since it invalidates the will of man. This view was expressed by one of the Catholic leaders who laid down guidelines for Catholic politics. See Appendix I.

6.   Bachem I, pp. 171 ff.

7.   "However painful the Divine edict, from the point of view of intent, it contains the element of redemption, and will redeem us the more if we acknowledge and recognize and derive benefit from the Divine intent behind the edict..." quoted in Bachem I, p. 42.

7a.   On the history of the Historische-Politischen Blaetter, see Haase p. 38ff, p. 63ff.

8.   Schnabel IV p. 207.

8a.   Hertz, p. 181/2.

9.   Lill in Rengstorf, pp. 371-375.

10.   "It is worth acknowledging the fact that the relations which have prevailed till now between church and state have crumbled completely and that it is also impossible to maintain ties in any other framework. The establishment of a new framework is an urgent need. This is our mission, which permits no solution but this, to proclaim the independence of the community of the faithful. The religious organization should be entrusted with the conduct of its own affairs, as is the case with all other associations." From Bergstrasser, p. 163.

11.   Sterling, p. 56.

12.   Greive, *Theologie*, p. 22.

24

13.　　On the essence of the Christian sermon, see Karl Barth: "The sermon is the task which the church imposes on those chosen to serve it, to explain that which was written in the Scriptures to the people of today, in such clear language that they will understand those matters pertaining to them, as if they were hearing directly the Divine message." In Homiletik, Vorlesungsnachschrift, in: Barth, Karl.

14.　　Schnabel IV, p. 44.

15.　　Heinz-Mohr, p. 10; pp. 203-204; the author presents colourful sermons, marked by folk humour.

16.　　This was written by Dr. Schöpf, a senior dignitary of the Church, in the Wiener Kalender in 1896. Quoted in Bloch, p. XLVII "Hatred and revulsion are implanted in the heart of the child while he is still small...He is told horror tales of blood-suckers and blood libels....The kindly grandmother takes her grandchild to the Jewstone at Hal (on the Inn plain) and points to the cruel features. The child is intimidated and cannot free himself of the fearful image....The face of the Jew is distorted to the point where doubts are raised as to whether Jews are human... On the Karfreitag, the day of the Crucifixion, the Perfidi Judaei prayer is recited. What does the priest, particularly the pious one, think when reading these words: he surely thinks, he must think that the church itself, in its very hymns, abhors the Jews as *perfidia gens*, and thus our pious man, nolens volens, becomes an antisemite."

The Hal blood libel of 1462, to which Schöpf refers, appeared in 1889 in the fourth edition of a book of stories for kindergartens, pp. 382-386. See translation in Appendix.

17.　　Homily: in the narrow sense- rhetoric in the Holy tongue. In the wider sense-the theory of the sermon.

18.　　Patiss, Introduction.

19.　　Schmuelling, Vol 2, p. 241 f.

CHAPTER FOUR

THE OLD TESTAMENT AS HARBINGER OF CHRISTIANITY

The Sunday sermons drew their catechistic content from the Old and New testaments. According to this catechism, these sermons, without exception, denied the intrinsic value or primacy of the Old Testament. The preachers emphasized the transiency of the Jewish Scriptures, whose only task was to serve as the harbinger of the true faith, Christianity. This view of the functional - and hence temporal - value of the Scriptures, contains an element of positive evaluation of the Jewish religion. It was perceived as the mirror of Christianity and the corridor leading to the truth, and this constitutes recognition of its value, however relative and fleeting. At the 1848 Wuerzburg assembly, the bishops compared the church to Israel, and expressed great esteem for the biblical tales and for the prophets.[1] On their scale of values, the Bible was placed between the invalid beliefs of the idol worshippers and the Christian doctrines. Christianity, as a 'more elevated and noble 'religion, is at the pinnacle.[2] Paganism was relegated to the bottom of the scale, from which it was possible to rise only with the support of Judaism. This historical process was often mentioned in sermons. The positive evaluation of the Jewish religion was based on its ability to inculcate in the pagans belief in one sole Redeemer. The sojourn of the Children of Israel in Egypt and their journey through the desert, were interpreted as an expression of the Divine will, so that the idol-worshippers would accept the Holy Scriptures, and particularly belief in the future advent of the Messiah.[3] It was declared that words cannot suffice to describe the superiority of the

Jewish people over the ancient peoples described in the Old Testament."[4]
An 1888 apologetic essay by Weiss[*] on Christianity, comparing Jewish and
pagan customs, is illustrative of the attitude of respect for Judaism. The
author compared the institution of marriage in ancient Greece and in biblical
Israel, and deplored the Greek concept of family life. He wrote: "The
greatest weakness of the Greek people....this is a monstrous affair which runs
against nature (*grauenvolle Unnatur*), which would never have become a
national epidemic were it not for that desecration of marriage which became
the disease of the entire people."[5]

Referring to Jewish family life, he expressed the reservation, so
characteristic of Catholic churchmen: "In contrast to these (i.e. Greek Z.B.)
phenomena - our glimpse of the internal conditions of the Jewish people is
an inspiration (*Geisteserhebung*). However, they too did not achieve purity
according to Christian criteria, such as we would have wished to see."[6] Of
the pagans he declared that in order to justify their shame (*Schande*), they
had cast their sweet abomination (*Suesse Laester*) on their gods. The Jews, in
contrast, punished sinners with death. The ancient peoples authorized the
paterfamilias to sentence his children to life or death, while the Torah laws
defended them against arbitrary authority, but sentenced the rebellious son
to death. The Hellenes perceived marriage as a political institution, serving
the good of the polis, while in the Old Testament the demands of the state
took second place to the good of the individual.[7]

Concerning the status of women and their honour in Judaism, he
declared "that in ancient times, only Judaism guarded the honour of women,"
but immediately added, "in modern times, this is the right of Christianity
alone."[8]

Christianity and Judaism were close in their advocacy of belief in one
God. Moses was compared to Jesus, since both were considered emissaries
of God, though Jesus's superiority was presupposed, and required no proof.
The uncompromising value judgment as to the superiority of Christianity
over Judaism was expressed in various forms. For example, in discussions of
houses of prayer, the church was described as a holy place. "Holier than the
Burning Bush, than Mount Sinai, and holier than the Temple in Jerusalem,
for those holy places were ideals for the Christian temple."[9] This is a striking

example of the dialectical process into which Judaism was integrated. It is superior to paganism and inferior to Christianity and, paradoxically, this same inferiority becomes an indispensable condition of the Christian religion. The paradox is anchored in almost all homiletic literature. Easter is a nobler festival of freedom than the Jewish Passover; the prophet Isaiah, according to a preacher from Augsburg, prophesied the fate of Jesus, his death and sanctification.[10]

The quoting of the Jewish Scriptures was justified on the grounds that they could teach the faithful about 'the emergence of the Christian religion.'[11]

Of the Jewish people as the people of the Bible it was said that they served 'as testimony, through their humiliation and decline, to the truth of Christianity."[12]

The paradox is strikingly evident in the statement by one of the preachers that 'the New Testament is the realization of the Old Testament."[13]

In priestly sermons, the motif of the Old Testament as the ideal and the harbinger of Christianity is often reiterated, particularly in references to the image and personality of Jesus. Various Old Testament characters were quoted as tokens of the life and personality of Jesus. For example, in the history of Abel, preachers sought indications of the destiny of Jesus. Just as Abel fell victim to the envy and hatred of his brother, Cain, "thus Jesus was killed by his blood brothers, the Jews."[14]

The High Priest, sitting in the Holy of Holies, which is compared to Heaven, is a sign of the advent of Jesus, since, in offering up sacrifices, he is alluding to the sacrifice of Jesus.[15]

The canvas was extended, so that not only the holy rituals performed by the High Priest, but all sacrifices in the Bible "were, without exception, tokens"[16] of Jesus, and all of them together were weighed against his one great sacrifice. On the other hand, it is interesting to note, in this context, that other views were also expressed. Mehler, a well-known catechist, stated that the sacrifices in the Old Testament must disappear, but that it could not be argued that all of them were balanced against the sacrifice of Jesus since, according to Christian tradition, his was a one-time sacrifice in Jerusalem alone. Adam, the first man created, was seen by Christian thinkers as a token of the advent of Jesus, a 'man in spirit' (First Epistle to the Corinthians, 15, 45)[17] Noah was seen as a sign of the coming of Christ. The Ark was perceived as a symbol of the church, and the flood - as the sign of baptism.[18]

The sacrifice of Isaac was the symbol of the Crucifixion, and Joshua, who led the Children of Israel to the promised land, was compared to Jesus, who redeemed mankind by leading them from the wilderness of this world to the blessings of the next world.[19]

The various acts of heroism mentioned in the Bible were also related to the miraculous actions of Jesus. The valour of Gideon and his three hundred men (Judges 7, 19-21) was interpreted as allusions to the future appearance of Jesus, accompanied by a small band of followers, the Disciples. His deed is a sign of the love of God, which will eventually lead to the triumph of the Christian redeemer over his hostile surroundings. The birth and deeds of Samson served as a token of the wondrous birth of Christ. His choice of a wife was interpreted as a symbol of the growth of the church. His death, which caused the downfall of the Philistines, was explained as an allegory for the crucifixion of Christ which, according to Christian tradition, was intended to confound Satan.[20] Connections were also sought between the scriptural texts and other figures sacred to Christianity. Eve was compared to Mary, mother of Jesus and Sarah, wife of Abraham was depicted as the symbol of the church of Christ.[21] Signs and tokens were discovered not only in biblical characters, but also in events, places and inanimate objects. Thus, for example, the tree of life in the Garden of Eden , and the wooden logs prepared for the sacrifice of Isaac are tokens of the cross.[22] The brass serpent which Moses placed in the desert to save the Children of Israel from the bite of the fiery serpents (Numbers 21, 6-9), was compared to Jesus on the cross at whom the believers gazed in order to save themselves from the temptations of Satan.[23] As regards the Sabbath, an interpretation was adopted which denied the sanctity which the Jews attributed to the day. It was argued that "the day of the Lord is not intended for Jews but for Christians, for whom it was consecrated by the resurrection of our Lord."[24]

These examples can suffice to illustrate the Catholic approach to the Scriptures. This is not the appropriate framework for discussion of the methods of disputation and defence, and the Jewish reaction to these theories. Let it suffice to note that Jewish scholars pointed out the weaknesses and drawbacks of this method of interpretation, which removed Scriptures from their true context in order to adapt them to the Christian message.[25] For our purposes, the important fact is that Christian preachers acknowledged the value of the Old Testament, as Jewish testimony. The above-mentioned Josef Deharbe expressed this attitude of respect, albeit with reservations. After declaring that the Divine truth had been transferred from the Jews - the most bitter enemies of Christianity - to the Christians, and that Divine providence had allotted the Jewish people the historical status of a humiliated nation, as symbol and testimony to the triumph and superiority of Christianity - he asked a rhetorical question: "How can the truth prevail in the end when the beginning is deception?" To believe that the Holy Scriptures were a deception, would have destroyed the basis of Christianity. Hence, Deharbe concluded that the Catholic Church must acknowledge the truth of both the Old and the New Testaments.[26] In line with this trend, other Catholic theologians lauded the Old Testament, for example singling out for approval the social justice underlying the laws of the Torah.[27] According to Deharbe, the laws and precepts of the Torah were given so that men could learn and understand the deeds of the Creator and the Divine attitude towards this world. He conceded that observance of the Torah precepts could preserve a man from sin.[28]

The answer to Deharbe's rhetorical question embodies the entire problem of the attitude of the Catholic church towards Judaism. On the basis of what has been quoted so far, one might have expected the Christian church to respect Judaism, because of the affinity of faith. If tradition is not 'deception', if the content of the Jewish scriptures is worthy of respect whence sprang the denial? As the answer reveals, the Old Testament was sanctified and esteemed by Christians, -but this esteem was hedged wit. reservations. Its content was considered moral, inasmuch as it brought about good. It is not intrinsically good -since, according to this approach it is

30

imperfect - good is contained only in the New Testament, in which the Divine
mission will be realized in full.

However, it was difficult for the preachers to use the word 'imperfect
in reference to the Old Testament. If they acknowledged it, even if only as a
guide to the true and the good, then - so a certain preacher argued - they
were essentially acknowledging the Jews as 'the spiritual masters of the
world'.[29] Since Christianity accepted the message of the Old Testament and
the teachings of the prophets, (albeit with qualified approval), as well as the
fact that the Jews believed 'in one true God who created heaven and earth'
and believed in the coming of the Messiah - they were accorded a certain
respect by some circles within the Catholic clergy.[30] These attitudes,
however, related to the biblical reality. Later, as will be seen below, a clear
distinction was drawn between biblical Jews and modern Jews.

In the context of the Scriptures, it was even claimed that Christians
should take an example from the religious conduct of the Jews, who never
uttered the name of God, except in prayer, and then only with great
reverence. Not only the obligations of man towards God, but also the mutual
aid were praised by Catholic thinkers and institutions. The attitude to slaves
as expressed in the Old Testament was singled out for approbation. It was
described as unique in the ancient world, since Jews were ordered to work
beside their slaves and to grant them a weekly day of rest. The laws of the
Torah also stipulated that certain basic rights of slaves be recognized. These
facts were pointed out by one of the important leaders of German Catholics,
Emmanuel Ketteler, Bishop of Mainz, who was known for his struggle to win
equal rights for Christian workers. Although he condemned the stubborn
refusal of the Jews to acknowledge Christ, and considered their historical
situation to be evidence of the superiority of Christianity, he did not hesitate
to laud them for their way of life which was marked by social justice, based
on their laws.[31]

In one of the catechistic compilations for schools, the author
described an act of grace performed by a Jew who had been subjected to
mockery and torture by a Christian. Later, the Jew rescued the child of his
persecutor from a fire. Through this unusual example, the author sought to

show that the Jews were bound by the precepts of the Torah to love their fellow-men.[32]

This example is exceptional, and has no parallel in homiletic, literature and sermons. Moreover, various sources indicate that this praise of the generous Jew was rare, and Jews were usually viewed with skepticism and suspicion. This can be learned, inter alia, from an incident which occurred in one of the small towns of Germany.[33]

The above-mentioned view of biblical characters and the concept of the transient role of the Jewish people, remained the dominant outlooks. In the end they led to the devaluation of Jews in the eyes of Christian believers. 'Transient justice' and 'transient morality' are unacceptable terms. One might even say that 'transient morality' is, at core, not moral all. But it was necessary to find proof, or to invent a persuasive argument, for the 'transient' existence of the biblical Jew.

32

NOTES

1.   Lill, in Rengstorf, p. 371.

2.   Diessel, p. 622; "When the Redeemer appeared...the Jewish religion ceased to be the true religion....the respect which the Jews had bestowed on the Creator, was a mere illusion. Now it yielded place to the substance. Its place was taken by a more noble and superior religion."

3.   Knoll, Vol 1, p. 62; "The Jewish people were shaped as a nation of priests... this, in order to preserve among the pagans and idol-worshipper the faith in one God and in redemption."

Wenzel, p. 59: "Through contact with the Jews who lived amidst the pagan peoples, they learned of the faith in the true God and of the messianic prophesies."

4.   Koerber, p. 12.

5.   Weiss, p. 396.

6.   *Ibid, ibid*.

7.   *Ibid, ibid*. The author quotes Numbers 20, 7;24, 5.

8.   *Ibid*, p. 451.

9.   Huller, p. 212.

10.   For the prophet Isaiah prophesied long since the fate of our Divine redeemer, his birth from the virgin womb...his death and his elevation, from Abbt, p. 21.

11.   Deharbe/2, p. 484. Josef Deharbe (1800-1870), born in Strassburg, Jesuit priest, was an authority on the Catholic catechism. His book "Katholischer Katechismus oder Lehrbegriff" was widely disseminated in the bishoprics of Cologne Mainz, Paderborn, Fulda, Ermninland, Culm, Gniesen-Posen.

12.   *Ibid*, p. 130.

13.   Rolfus, p. 775.

14.   Lierheimer, p. 226.

15.   Gradaus, p. 53.

16.   "All the sacrifices...with and without blood...related without exception Jesus the Messiah, and were signs of the great sacrifice which Jesus mad on the Cross." From Zollner, p. 56.

17.   Koerber, p. 17ff.

18.   Deharbe/1, p. 23.

19.   Kroenes, Vol 9, 1860, p. 125.

20.   *Ibid, ibid.*

21.   Koerber, p. 17ff.

22.   Diessel, Vol 2, p. 186ff.

23.   Kroenes, Vol 9, pp. 126-7.

24.   Kroenes, Vol II, 1861, p. 168.

25.   We note here only two Jewish polemical works: Guttmann, Eschelbacher.

26.   Deharbe/2, p. 130;203;230.

27.   In Christlich-Soziale Blaetter (CSB), paper founded in 1868 due to the increasing influence of the working class.   In the sixties, von Ketteler initiated the establishment of workers associations in the Rhine and Ruhr areas. The 'Christian socialist' views found expression in this paper. In 1876 a series of articles appeared under the heading 'The Social Legislation of the Jews' praising biblical social justice. Of the jubilee year, it was said there: "The jubilee year is a social institution aimed at maintaining equality among landowners. It prevents excessive land purchase on the one hand and fragmentation on the other." On respect for human beings and the aspiration for equality, it wrote "that among the Jews the supreme dignity of man is universally expressed and acknowledged. Their religion does not recognize class distinctions: the House of Israel is one single family created by one God...all are united under one law." In Christliche-Soziale Blätter, No. 2, p. 42; No. 10, 1876, p. 74.

28.   Deharbe/2, p. 484.

29.   Gradaus, p. 137: "It is not true that Christianity is the perfect Judaism If this were so, the Jews would be the spiritual masters of the world." It interesting to note, in this context, the remarks of the Protestant Bruno Bauer in his essay 'The Jewish question'. He admits that "Christianity is the complement of Judaism, that Christian morality is the consistent observance of Jewish morality, that the views of human society are the outcome of the Jewish world outlook - but since Christianity complements Judaism, it inevitably also denies the Jewish essence." Bauer, p. 79.

34

30.   Schmidt, p. 235.

31.   "Jewish slavery is unique in all the ancient world, as is the concept of work as perceived by the Jews. The Jew worked beside his slave and granted him his weekly day of rest just like his own fellow-Jews, and he was obliged to respect the basic human rights of his slave." Ketteler, p. 458.

32.   Der Praktische Katechet, p. 53.

33.   In September 1879, a fair was held in Bischofsburg to collect funds for charitable institutions....after the priest's sermon, someone proposed donating a small house...Do you know who gave this gift? It was a Jew...but where are nine others to do the same?

CHAPTER FIVE

THE BIBLICAL JEW VERSUS THE MODERN JEW

Since the Catholic church - because of its own specific needs - could not leave its followers in a state of uncertainty and ambivalence towards the Jews and their beliefs, and since its policy was to present a total view of the inferiority of the Jew, it was obliged to indicate where this inferiority was manifested in the Old Testament, Christian respect for the content of the scriptures notwithstanding. This clarification is important, since it helps explain how the negative image of the Jew became entrenched over the centuries.

Catholic exegesis, in its efforts to demonstrate the paltriness of the Jews, did not hesitate to distort the meaning and significance of various texts. The result was far from complimentary to the image of the Jew, and helped to disseminate negative stereotypes. The following few examples illustrate the type of message directed by preachers at their audiences. The entry 'funeral' in the above- mentioned manual for preachers and religious instructors *Handgebrauch fuer Prediger und Religionslehrer*), notes that the Hebrews buried their dead a long time after death occurred. The reason cited for the delay was that "inter alia, they could not take their leave of the property connected to the deceased person, and only an advanced state of putrefaction and danger of a health hazard forced them to do so." To substantiate this claim, they referred to the story of Sarah, wife of Abraham, who "only after seven days was buried by Abraham (Genesis 23, 19)."[1] This is a blatant falsehood, since these words do not appear in the verse cited. If such statements appeared in the 'Real-lexikon', described as 'the most suitable material for the preacher of the Catholic faith,'[2] nobody was likely to check their veracity, since the scientific authenticity of the text was considered unquestionable. These despicable remarks about Abraham present him as the archetype of the Jew who "finds his happiness in materiality."[3] For generations to come, Jews would bear the burden of this negative mirage.

The lexicon goes on to explain the Jewish custom of locating burial places close to settlements and close to the synagogue "so that they can see the cemetery from their homes, for this sight warns them of their own approaching death." This interpretation, which has no substantiation in the scriptures, implies that it was not respect for the dead but mortal dread, the expression of a gloomy and self-centered faith, which motivated the Jews. This image was imprinted on the minds of the Christian audience. However, it should be emphasized, these explanations and descriptions, for better or worse, relate to the scriptures alone, mainly as theological commentaries, and are not related to the image of the modern Jew. The question is how these preachers explain the source of these so-called negative traits, the 'Jewish materialism' which they consider to be reflected in the Bible? The answer can be found in the Catholic view of the Jewish attitude towards the law, the written injunctions in the Torah. The Jews were described as not merely observing the religious law, but as slaves to it. According to this argument, the written word had killed the spirit. The rigid adherence to the letter of the law, had suppressed the aesthetic spirit. It was categorically declared that the Torah laws were 'of debased and materialistic nature.'[4] The heavy yoke of the written word had caused "the death of the spirit and worship of the formal letter."[5] This narrow outlook - it was argued in one of these sermons - had stifled the inspiration and talent of the Jew for artistic and scientific creativity, since his restricted perceptions barred him from liberating and creative experience.[6] Because of this blind acceptance of the 'dead' word, and strict adherence to petty detail, the Jews were now characterized by a narrow outlook, hypocrisy and pretence, in short, what some scholars define as Jewish legalism. The attack on Jewish legalism was not confined to Catholics. Protestantism also condemned it utterly. From the Reformation onward, strict adherence to the written text was considered a superficial and invalid manifestation of faith, since it remained within the sphere of mere formalism. The inner experience, the drive towards the inner truth, the faith of the heart - all these, the reformists believed, were totally at odds with legal- formalistic obedience.[7]

According to the Christian critique, the hypocrisy stemmed from the uncompromising insistence that the written law be scrupulously obeyed, and it was this inflexibility which aroused counter-reaction in the Jews. In other words, it aroused in them the urge to liberate themselves from the bonds of the law. The Jew -thus Emmanuel Ketteler claimed, was powerless (er war ohnmaechtig) to obey the law literally, and thus, he often castrated the text (entstellte) or escaped into idolatry."[8] The Christian theory denied the inherent moral content of law and mitzva, and perceived them merely as encouragement for the soul of man to acknowledge his sin, imperfection, and need to prepare himself for the spiritual salvation which only Jesus could bestow. Mere observance of the law exposed human frailty. The Jew, through being willing only to respect the written law, and by his refusal to acknowledge Jesus as the Messiah, was increasing his own sinfulness and hastening his perdition.[9]

Catholic theology established connections between the Jew, his beliefs and his actions, and sin. Moreover - it barred him from divine redemption and left him on earth with all his corporal lusts and weaknesses.

And, indeed, in Christian literature in general, in theological writings, in lexicons and books of instruction for teachers, preachers and pupils, the Jew was depicted as materialistic, his gaze fixed only on earthly, material objects. This trait was usually shown as related to his inflexible observance of the law, or as a result of strict insistence on its implementation. We hear for example that "the people who believe that they were directed by law, are called a synagogue, which means an assembly, since beasts, in their lust for corporal things, must be assembled together hence, rightly, the Christian people are denoted not synagogue but church, since they despise the corporal objects of mortal beings, and aspire only to the celestial and the eternal."[10] Jesus - so they claimed - felt out of place in this material world.

38

"It is not the wish of Jesus to learn from the Old Testament, for the tenets of his teachings are utterly different (grundverschieden) - they are in conflict with Judaism."[11]

The Catholic church offered its believers, in dogmatic and systematic fashion, a biblical world, in which the sinful and inferior image of the Jew is manifested. The social justice reflected in the Bible attests to the grandeur of God, but not to the sterling character of the Jew. Attachment to the letter of the law, according to Catholic interpretation, had fostered in the Jews the qualities of inflexibility (starrer sklavischer Sinn), of absence of understanding and of cheapness. Every Jew, it was claimed, sinned through his very Judaism. They sought the sign of this sinning in circumcision, and this will be discussed below.

The image of the Jew as perceived by the Christian believer, was influenced by various factors, dwelt upon by the preachers in church sermons.

Firstly -a Jew who failed to abide by the law, became a sinner. Secondly - circumcision was a sign of sinfulness. Thirdly - the Jew could be saved, if he accepted Jesus as his redeemer from sin.

Let us examine how these ideas were presented. Jesus, the divine figure, took on the form of a man in order to reveal himself to the people, who were groaning under the yoke of law and mitzvot, in order to liberate them from subjugation to the law. For the Jew, circumcision is a covenant symbolizing the fact that he has become a member of a congregation which abides by certain laws and precepts. Through this act, he expresses his submission and desire to obey the laws imposed on him. The advent of Christ changed the significance of circumcision. "Why was Jesus circumcised? Circumcision is the sign of subjection to divine law. And what is it if not the expression of obedience? Circumcision was part of redemption, for therein are manifested suffering and bloodshed. Jesus, through his suffering, redeemed the world....Circumcision symbolizes the divine shedding of blood - from the beginning to the crucifix."[12]

As saviour, Jesus was obliged to accept the 'mark of sin' (Merkmal der Suende) since, otherwise, he could not have appeared as one who accepted the curse of sin in order to atone for sinners. Hence,- argued the preachers - he was circumcised.[13]

This Christian explanation confronts Christian circumcision with Jewish circumcision. The former liberates man from the yoke of the religious precepts, the narrow confines of the law, through the spirit and grace bestowed by Christ the redeemer. It cleanses the Jew of the sin of egalism and of corporeality. The latter - forces and constrains the Jew within the narrow limits of acceptance of the yoke of the kingdom of Heaven, where he promises to observe the law and the precepts.[14] Catholics, loyal to their faith, demanded 'circumcision of the heart' instead of 'bodily circumcision". "If we receive the grace of the imparting of the Holy Spirit through baptism, what need is there of 'bodily circumcision'?[15]

This approach attests to the accusatory approach of Christians seeking to detach Christianity from Judaism. They admit that Christianity originated in Judaism, but their objective is liberation from Judaism. As the superior and prevailing force, Christianity holds out a hand to its sinful mother to redeem it and bring it to the true religion The polarity between Jesus, the good, the divine saviour, and the sinful and corporal Jew is inevitable. The argument that the Jew inherited his corruption from his own inacceptable attitude to religious law, bolstered the Christian belief in the primeval sin, inherent in Jews since biblical times.

It was not the crucifixion of Christ which caused the Jew to be despised and reviled. This was considered the consequence of his inherent corruption. It was not the historical reality of the despicable deed which indicated the character of the Jews, but the dry and barren legalism which had corrupted their nature. This is the rule determining relations between Christian and Jews: it was not history which shaped the Jewish character, but rather that same character which moved history.

Since the explanation for the inferior nature of the Jewish character had been found, it is not surprising to note that Jewish character was attacked more than Jewish tradition. Crudely enough, a distinction was drawn between the Jew as 'persona non grata' and the biblical tradition which, at least relatively speaking, was accorded positive recognition by Christians. It is no chance that in modern times, the most virulent attacks have been levelled against the 'Talmudic Jews' rather than 'the Jews of the Bible'.

40

This reverence for the Bible, and acknowledgement of the sanctity of the Old Testament for Christianity, has become, paradoxically enough, one of the elements of modern anti-semitism. I say paradoxically, because the praise lavished on the books of the Bible as the source of Christian morality, has served as the pretext in modern times for differentiation between the biblical Jew and the despised modern Jew, who was identified with the 'Talmudic' Jew. This subject will be discussed at greater length below. The drawing of this distinction was based on inference of the negative from the positive. On the basis of the positive values which were acknowledged to be inherent in the Bible, and there alone, negative qualities were inferred in the modern Jew. This distinction was pointed out by Cardinal Michael von Faulhaber, Archbishop of Munich, in his critique of the Nazi approach to Christianity. His remarks were made in 1933, shortly after Hitler came to power, and hence had a vital impact on the fate of the Jews under the Third Reich. In his sermons, delivered in the Church of St. Michael and published in 1934 under the title "Judaism, Christianity and Germanity" he drew three distinctions. First, he stated "we must distinguish between the Jewish people before the death of Christ and afterwards. Before the death of Christ, in the era of Abraham's mission...it was the sons of Israel who bore the divine revelation. The Holy Spirit elevated and illuminated the countenance of people who established their religious and civil life according to the laws of Moses....after His death, Israel was deprived of the sacred worship of the religion of the Revelation....they denied and rejected God's Messiah....Secondly, we must distinguish between the word of the Old Testament on the one hand, and the words of the Talmud of Judaism after Christ, on the other....I am referring in particular to the Talmud, the Mishna, the edicts of the Middle Ages and the Shulhan Arukh. The books of the Talmud are the work of man; they were not composed under divine inspiration. Only the holy writings of the pre-Christian era, and not the Talmud, were accepted as a heritage by the church of the New Testament. And thirdly, we must distinguish within the Old Testament between enduring values and fleeting ones by undertaking to sanctify the holy scriptures, Christianity did not become a Jewish religion....these books were not written by the Jews; they were composed under the inspiration of the Holy Spirit."

This statement was considered both courageous and honorable, since the Cardinal was attacking the Nazi approach which denied the existence of any Jewish traces in Christianity, whether preceding it or following it. But, on the other hand, he remained faithful to the Catholic tradition, which stamped modern Jews with the mark of shame and of contempt. Thus, indirectly, he was granting legitimization to Nazi assaults on the modern Jews. This is a fascinating example of the continuous line of traditional-Christian anti-Jewishness, which, for generations, has nurtured haters of Jews.[16]

NOTES

1.   Kroenes, Vol 11, 1856, p. 90.

2.   *Ibid., ibid.*

3.   Gradaus, p. 70.

4.   Koerber, p. 45: "The Children of Israel... bore the yoke of the Torah precepts, a yoke of harsh and humiliating decrees...laws of debased and materialistic nature..."

5.   *Ibid.,* p. 10. This is based John, 1, 17: "For the Law was given by Moses, but grace and truth came by Jesus Christ."

6.   Ehrler, p. 27. The French philosopher, Ernest Renan arrived at similar conclusions. In his essay "L'Histoire Générale et Système Comparé des Langues Sémitiques, Paris, 1848, he referred to the sémitic spirit" in which the monothéistic tendencies of the Jews were stamped.

7.   Deharbe/l, p. 398. It is worth noting the emergence of the concept of "legalism". Modern research has noted that the term appeared in he nineteenth century, and that in earlier centuries (16th and 17th) the argument was unknown. Its emergence is explained as resulting from the new trend to focus on the personality of Jesus, and one of the ways is to present the narrow character of the Jew, as the antithesis of the spiritual nature of Jesus. This theory is borne out by the use of the 'legalistic' argument in numerous sermons. It is worth quoting the remarks of Moore, pp. 197-254.

"...The characterization of Judaism in nineteenth-century German scholarship is strikingly different from the older apologetic and polemic....So it is also with the 'legalism' which, for the last fifty years has become the very definition and the all-sufficient condemnation of Judaism. It is not a topic of the older polemic; indeed, I do not recall a place where it is even mentioned...What then brought legalism to the front in the new apologetics?...The 'essence' of Christianity, and therefore its specific difference from Judaism, was for the first time sought in the religion of Jesus - his teachings and his personal piety...the 'Father in heaven', the piety assumed to be distinctive of Jesus and of his teaching, demanded an antithesis in Judaism, an inaccessible God."

And see also Paul R. Mendes-Flohr: Ambivalent Dialogue: Jewish Christian Theological Encounter in the Weimar Republic, in Kulka, especially p. 113.

On Protestant opposition see the discussion of Erasmus of Rotterdam in Oberman, p. 40.

8.   Ketteler, p. 51.

9.   Kuhn, p. 23. On the gap between this approach and the Jewish outlook, see Hans Joachim Schoeps, pp. 49-61.

10.   Kroenes, Vol 8, 1859, p. 362.

11.   Mehler, p. 567.

12.   Koerber, p. 52.

13.   Zollner, p. 107.

This approach bases itself on the verse: "Hear, O my people and I will speak. O Israel and I will testily against thee. I am God, even thy God" (Psalms 50, 7).

14.   Koerber, p. 53 and Kroenes, Vol 9, 1869, p. 45.

15.   Koerber, *ibid.*, *ibid.* Christ's circumcision ceremony: For us (the Christians Z.B.), circumcision is an obligation or a call for spiritual circumcision, or the killing of the lust for evil. Jesus became the ideal through circumcision since he sacrificed freedom for obedience, pride for humility, pleasure for pain. Why was he circumcised? In order to teach obedience, and not to give the Jews a pretext to reject his teachings. And he also sought to prove that he was a descendant of Abraham, and also in order to nullify the teachings of Moses, and lastly - in order to accept a kind of sin that he could atone for with his own body..." In Kroenes, Vol 9, p. 45.

16.   On Faulhaber's sermons see: Lewy, p. 276.

CHAPTER SIX

WHY GERMANY?

Before continuing this survey of Jewish-Catholic relations, I feel that some clarification is required.

The facts presented so far relate to the Catholic catechism and instruction as a whole, and the views and statements quoted concerning the Jews and Judaism, were universally valid. While the arguments cited are taken from the German catechism, they were certainly not unique to Germany. The Catholic catechism concerning attitudes towards the Jews and their religion was more or less uniform in the various countries. A 1974 study, conducted in Rome and in Belgium,[1] was based on two Catholic institutions, the Pro Deo in Rome and the Louvain project in Belgium. This study presents data from various manuals of instructions - Spanish, Italian and French,- in which it is claimed that the Jews rejected Jesus because of their materialistic character.[2] The author writes, interestingly: "The sweeping statements just quoted are wholly at variance with the historical facts. In Jesus' time, most Jews in Judea and Galilee were far from wealthy, and they were not merchants and businessmen but artisans."[3] The author apparently failed to grasp the severe implications of this Christian claim. Hence, she attempted to refute the charges of Jewish materialism by citing historical facts, namely that there were few prosperous Jews at the time. But according to the sources referred to above, the cause of anti-Jewish calumny was not historical fact, but the corrupt nature of the Jews themselves, the origins of which were sought in the Scriptures.

Theologically speaking, there was little difference, in this respect, between the views of preachers in France, in Germany, or in any other country. For all of them, the prime influence was the catechism, which provided Christian believers with a single doctrinal framework, and Germany was no exception to the rule. But, nonetheless, I have chosen to present the specific German version of universal Catholic standpoints, for what I believe to be clear historical reasons.

As noted above, religious tension was always linked with anti-Jewishness and anti-semitism.[4] The history of Germany in the twentieth century is steeped in Jewish blood. Hatred of Jews reached a murderous peak which is without parallel in human history. Catholicism, through being intertwined with the course of German history, as noted above,[5] shared in the historical responsibility weighing on Germany. This fact, in itself, justifies the singling out of the German Catholic camp from universal Catholicism, in the frame of reference of the Jews and Judaism. Were it not for the Holocaust, there would probably be no valid reason for referring to a unique German Catholic attitude towards the Jews.

The Christian theological indictments against the Jews took on added force within the terrible reality of the Holocaust. Nazism, which has rightly been called an anti-Jewish revolution,[6] and which clearly defined its objectives with regard to the fate of the Jews - could not have perpetrated its crimes without the backing and cooperation of the German population at large. The Nazi demand for the physical extermination of the Jews would not have won approval and even active assistance, without the conviction of a large part of the population that the Jews were fair game. The Nazi regime endured for only twelve years. Could it, in so brief a span, have persuaded the masses that it was permissible to slaughter Jews. Logic rejects this idea. No human being gets up one fine morning and sets out to kill Jews, just because he is ordered to do so. The aversion to Jews and everything related to them, was the outcome of education, of a lengthy tradition and of propaganda, dating back to long before the Holocaust.

Catholicism, which proclaims itself the bearer of the Divine truth, played a decisive role in fostering the negative image of the Jew. It would be difficult to pinpoint any direct connection between the Christian outlook and

Nazi atrocities. The Catholic church never advocated murder of the Jews. It would also be difficult to prove that the Nazis were influenced by Catholic anti-Jewish theology. But is essential to expose the transmission and absorption of the false, preconceived notions, which prevailed among the German people as the outcome of Catholic upbringing.

In Germany, some 23 years after the Holocaust, the following was said: "The catastrophe had two dimensions for Germans. Some Germans died a martyr's death during the persecution. Hence, the many were led to understand the fate of the Jews in a new light. This is one dimension of the catastrophe. The second is this: it is clear to every Christian today, that almost all of those who drove the innocent and the defenseless to their deaths, in almost inconceivable numbers, were the products of what may be denoted a 'Christian' education."[7] Raul Hilberg, who wrote a monumental study of the genocide of Jews in Europe, declared at the outset of his book that Hitler spoke to the people 'in a familiar language'.[8] This ideological affinity was not born out of a vacuum. In order to understand its roots, we must look back to the nineteenth century. German nationalism was crystallized in that period, and one of its main components was anti-semitism.[9] It has already been stated that the annals of the church as a social body, and the development of Catholicism as a manifestation of civilization, must be judged in the context of the laws of historical development.[10] The German regime assimilated the Catholic heritage, just as Catholicism operated within the tenets of the regime. Christian anti-Judaism merged with political anti-semitism. This atmosphere affected both the priesthood and their Catholic masses, and in due course polarization turned into hatred. The attitude of Catholics towards Jews fluctuated in accordance with prevailing political outlooks. But even when the official policy was restrained and moderate due to political considerations, Jews were always regarded with suspicion, particularly in rural areas,[11] where the congregation was directly influenced by sermons from the pulpit.

NOTES

1.   Bishop.

2.   "The Jewish people rejected Jesus in his lifetime: why did they do so? Out of materialism..." A French textbook claims: "...The unbelieving Jews...were too attached to money honors, the pleasure of life, to embrace a doctrine of self-denial" (AL.202: 12:199) p. 22. "The Jews were mercantile businessmen, little disposed to listen to Jesus" (PD.49:4), p. 22.

3.   *Ibid*, p. 23.

4.   Greive, Theology, p. 14.

5.   Moody, p. 1.

6.   Mosse, Nazism, p. 45.

7.   Rengstorf, Vol I, p. 18.

8.   Hilberg, p. 8.

9.   Almog, Anti-semitism.

10.   Moody, p. 331. Catholicism must be seen essentially as a reality belonging to the realm of historical and cultural phenomena."

11.   Rengstorf, Vol 2, p. 371; "The age-old aversion to the Jews was religiously motivated....It was particularly evident in rural areas." See above, Chap. 4, Note 1.

CHAPTER SEVEN

FROM THEOLOGY TO IDEOLOGY

Discussing the differences between the Christian and Jewish beliefs, David Flusser quotes the Jewish philosopher Franz Rosenzweig.[1]   For Christians, wrote Rosenzweig in his book *Stern das Erlösung*, faith is the content of witness, it is faith something. And thus it is the complete opposite of the faith of the Jew, which is not the content of evidence but the consequence of birth.   Whoever is born a Jew attests to his faith by augmenting the Eternal People. He does not have faith something, he *is* faith.

Flusser proffers the Jewish conviction that "not the Jewish religion but Israel itself" was chosen by God.   Therefore, he concludes, in dealing with Judaism, Christian theology should concern itself, not with the beliefs of the Jews, but with the Jewish people and their everlasting role as God's chosen people.[2]

This is the meaning of Rosenzweig's comment that the Jew "*is* faith".[3]

Had Catholic theology, catechism and dogma adopted this positive view of the Jewish faith, the entire Christian conception of Judaism would have been different. But in reality, the reverse occurred. It was not the Jewish religion as such, but those who professed it, the Jews as a chosen people, who were judged. But this interest in them did not stem from any objective desire to uncover the essence of the Jewish faith, but from opposition, of denial leading to hatred. The preachers did not depict the Jewish faith from the viewpoint of familiarity with its inner essence, or in a spirit of understanding, but rather judged Jewish customs and conduct according to Christian yardsticks. The result was that they placed the emphasis on the misdeeds of the Jews rather than their merits. This approach helped create a highly negative image of the Jew. Sermons and homiletic literature took as a central motif not the beliefs of the Jews, but their lack of faith, their heresy. The Jew was identified with sin and with apostasy. When preachers admonished Christians who had strayed from the path of faith, they compared them to the Jewish heretics, the symbol of sin.[4] Generally speaking, they quoted such expressions in the New Testament as "If I had not come and spoken unto them, they had not had sin: But now they have no cloak for their sin (John 15,22). Jewish heresy was presented to the congregation as adamant refusal to accept Jesus, this being the reason the Jews had been rejected by God.[5] It was no chance that John was frequently quoted. Research shows that the aim of the Gospel according to St. John was to narrate the life of Jesus after his resurrection, and hence it was written by a Christian and not by Jews in the days of early Christianity, before the resurrection. Later Christians, unlike their predecessors, rejected the source from which Christianity grew and regarded Judaism as a hostile entity.[6]

Jewish heresy and absence of faith were considered to stem from free will and choice. "The Lord abandoned this rebellious people to the calamity which they chose of their own will."[7] The Jews were accused even more blatantly in another sermon. "The source of their lack of faith is the fact that God does not force anyone not to believe, but leaves them the free alternative to choose what they wish, for better or worse."[8] And if the sin of heresy were not enough, the preachers believed that it had generated hatred of Christianity.

There is a difference between the view of the Jews as heretics and unbelievers, and the Jews as haters of Christianity. Heresy against Jesus and the Christian creed are matters for the individual, who arrives at his convictions through private calculations, and thus his personal perplexity is not actively extended to Christians as individuals. This is not the case with Jewish hatred. Its roots are generally emotional, and its impact is felt on external objects, outside the narrow confines of the Jewish world. The reactions of the Christian believer, whether based on spurious or valid arguments, were elicited by the words and deeds of the Jew. The lurid descriptions of the infinite hatred which Jews felt for Christians, roused an active anti-Jewish response, which was more intense than the response to Jewish heresy. In the eighteen fifties, the opinion was often voiced that the Jews should be granted emancipation, since this would put an end to Judaism, and consequently to Jewish hatred of Christianity.[9] Examination of sermons concerning Jewish hatred for Christians reveals that in few cases did they refer specifically to hostility towards Christianity as a creed and outlook. The hatred was usually depicted as directed against Jesus as an individual. The concrete and personalized accusations were more easily understood by the unlearned masses than were abstract arguments. By focusing on the figure of Jesus, the preachers could dwell on the historical event of the crucifixion. If, for example, we examine the Catholic catechism composed by Deharbe, we find, under 'hatred' the following remarks: "It was brotherly hatred which lured Cain to kill his brother, just as the Jews, out of open hatred, took up stones to stone Jesus (John 8, 59). The Pharisees hated Jesus because he reproached them as they deserved."[10] And another preacher added a dramatic touch, when he quoted a verse from Ben Sira: "He who throws up a stone, it will fall on his head..."(27, 28). This shifting of focus to the fate of Jesus at the hands of the Jews, intensified the hostile feelings of the Christian masses towards the Jews. The churchgoers absorbed such inflammatory statements as the following: "This satanic generation did not cease to be even when the Old Testament was forced to yield place to the New Testament. Even to the present day this Hell spawn endures, and the generation of the sacrilegious and the heretics have stolen from the Old Testament to the New and are proliferating eternally like poisonous weeds, and even among Christian communities..."[12] In other words: despite the triumph over Judaism, the despising and despised Jew still constitutes a very real threat to Christianity.

These negative characteristics of the Jews naturally led to their isolation among the nations. There could be two reasons for this seclusion: their own wishes, or external coercion by Christians. Throughout Jewish history, these two factors operated together. The voluntary separatism stemmed from Jewish religious customs led, on the one hand, to voluntary separatism, while Christian rejection condemned the Jews to seclusion within their own confined space and branded them with the mark of inferiority and shame. Christians were cautioned in sermons not to emulate Jews, and not to resemble them[13] for the Jews were considered fickle.[14] They were described as "miserable remnants, scattered throughout the world," and the churchgoers we exhorted to keep their distance from them. "Friends, have you any desire to be associated with this people who were rejected by the Creator?"[15] The Jews, in their isolation, were compared to "shallow rivers twisting and turning through deep, wide sea of other nations, and the flow of their waters has no force and cannot mingle with the waters of the great oceans, into which they flow."[16]

This Catholic approach created new historical realities. The collective vilification of the Jews as accursed sinners, caused them to be shunned by the rest of mankind. This isolation transformed the Jewish people into an unwanted vulnerable minority, fated to be ever dependent on the mercies of others, the target of the hostility of non-Jews in general, and Christians in particular.

Since the Jew was considered a heretic and a rebellious sinner, the basic tenets of his creed were utterly rejected. Particularly abhorred were Jewish messianic beliefs, which were interpreted in a manner inconsistent with both Jewish and Christian sources. This misrepresentation of Jewish messianism, on the one hand, and of Christian messianism on the other - has been pointed out by such scholars as David Flusser and Clemens Thoma.[17] The present study is not concerned with the scientific and theological aspects of this issue, but with the way in which these theological outlooks evolved into the set of prejudices reflected in sermons and in homiletic literature. To a certain extent, we are dealing with the vulgarization of Christian theology by the minor clergy.

The preachers (and the manuals of instruction they consulted) felt no need to understanding the profounder truths underlying the Jewish scriptural sources. For them, it was a historical and theological fact that Jesus was the Messiah, in total contradiction of the Jewish view. For them, the Jews had always been his sworn foes and consequently were also the enemies of Christianity as a whole. Jewish belief in the advent of the Messiah was rejected on the grounds that "apart from Jesus there is no Messiah: or should we adopt the belief of the modern Jew, that Judaism is the realization of messianism which will save the world?" It is the existential mission of Judaism "to serve, through its wondrous survival, as testimony to messianism, until the Day of Judgment arrives for all peoples on earth..."[18]

This theory that Catholic attacks on the Jews were grounded on ideological and not theological reasoning is borne out by the fact that the modern catechism has not concerned itself with Jewish doctrine, that is to say, has not judged the Jewish religion, but has focused on the personal angle, on the nature of the modern Jews. For the Christian, the Jew, in his everyday manifestation, as neighbour, was the personification of evil, and the origin of this evil was sought in the Jewish messianic falsehood. The only references to religion, are to "contemporary religion". It was said that" the contemporary Jewish religion, which still stubbornly awaits the coming of the Messiah - is grounded on error. For Christianity and not modern Judaism (emphasis mine. Z.B.) is the legitimate continuation of the true ancient Judaism. Contemporary Judaism can be compared to the husk which remains after the butterfly has emerged from the larva."[19]

In Catholic writings dealing with the modern Jew and his messianic beliefs, there is another underlying note, which is worthy of attention. Once Jews had been reproached for adhering to messianic beliefs, but now that the spirit of modernism had touched the Catholic rank-and-file, the obverse charge was levelled against him. Modern liberal trends were now identified with the Jewish spirit, since they too were thought to undermine conservative Catholic beliefs. Liberalism, which advocated progress, mocked both Christian and Jewish messianic beliefs.

This explained why the modern Jew, who had cast off the yoke of religion, had abandoned the messianic ideal and, in its stead, had been drawn to adopt the liberal outlook.

"We are no longer speaking of yearning for the Messiah's advent" since for the Jews "this belief is now pointless. They have cast off the yoke of law and of religious injunctions." According to this theory a new type of Jew has emerged: "the Jew without messianic beliefs."[20] Even among Protestants, who were less hostile towards liberalism than were Catholics, the modern Jews were sometimes denounced "for the divisive spirit of reform Judaism, which has turned its back on eschatological hopes."[21]

These contradictory Christian arguments indicate the totality of the opposition to Jews. In the end, even if this was not stated explicitly, the only hope for Jews lay in abandonment of their Judaism. Their creed was objectionable because of its messianic trends, and also because of its denial of true messianism. It is not surprising that this hostility intensified in the second half of the nineteenth century.

However, even those Jews who remained strictly observant, and continued to hold themselves apart from the society around them, were also the targets of Christian hostility. This seclusion was regarded as arrogant exclusivity, whereby they expressed their distaste for the misguided and inferior Christian world. This attitude, according to the preachers, stemmed from their rejection of Jesus as Messiah. Whereas the reformist Jews were seen as "worldly because of their attraction to modern needs, the "worldliness" of the traditional Jew was denounced because of his faith in the advent of the Messiah: "Messiah cannot be found here. The Jewish people anticipated the earthly kingdom of the Messiah, and the appearance of the monarch who will grant wealth and power...here and today."[22]

At the beginning of the twentieth century, the 'Protocols of the Elders of Zion' disseminated the anti-semitic theory that the Jews aspired to take over control of the world. But this socio-political charge was preceded by Catholic propaganda which linked the Jewish yearnings for the "messianic temporal kingdom" to their desire to dominate the world. Moreover, Norman Cohen has pointed out the existing connection between the legend of the Antichrist and the content of the Protocols: "There is no longer room for doubt. With all the force and terror of Satan, there comes the kingdom of the King of Israel who will conquer our world which is steeped in sin: a king born of the seed of Zion - the Antichrist - close to the universal throne of power..."[23] The identification of the Jewish Messiah with the Antichrist is found among Catholics in the mid nineteenth century. It is claimed that "the Jews are awaiting the Messiah, who will be revealed on the Day of Judgment and will bestow on them world domination....They will receive, according to the anointed one, a false Messiah and they will follow ardently in the path of the Antichrist..."[24]

These few examples suffice to demonstrate how theological elements were transformed over the centuries into ideology. This trend is particularly evident where messianism is concerned. The Jews, - so Catholic catechistic literature claims - envisage a Messiah characterized by wealth, splendor, power and a craving for domination. This is the antithesis of the ideal image of the Christian Messiah, marked by modesty, poverty and submissiveness.[24a] Later reproof of the Jews as exploiters, greedy and avid for gold and silver and greedy, derives from this theological argument: "The Jewish people awaited a temporal kingdom of the Messiah, and a rich and powerful king who would liberate them from Roman subjugation - and, as it was in the past, so it remains today."[25] As interpreted by Catholics, the Messiah's reign became the reign of Jewish wealth. The Messiah became the king of the stock exchange. What had once been perceived as the dominion of spiritual force, as the Divine will, was reduced deliberately to material power and Jewish avarice.[26]

We have noted that the priests could find support for their views in numerous manuals of instruction, including the various lexicons.[27] This literature reflected growing hostility towards the Jews, against the background of the anti-semitic trends which were intensifying at the turn of the century. In the past, Christians had sought to interpret the Jewish way of life in light of Jewish traditions and religious customs. In modern times, this Christian approach underwent modification. The Jews, it was now argued, had a "revolutionary spirit", and they were accused of subversiveness, whose origins were sought in their messianic outlook. Their revolutionary predilections stemmed from "false hopes fostered by the longed-for imminent arrival of the Messiah."[28] This revolutionary spirit was born out of their resentment at Christ's admonishments. Since then, "there is no rest for the eternal Jew, since there is no peace in him."[29]

The messianic idea was considered to be the cohesive force of Judaism till the emergence of reform Judaism in the nineteenth century. This trend, it was claimed, had distanced itself from the messianic ideal.[30] Hence, the reformists in particular were identified with modern Judaism as a whole, and with those socio-political trends which Catholics particularly abhorred, particularly in difficult times for Catholicism. Jews are active communists, it was said, because "the qualities of restlessness, of ferment, the attraction to new and revolutionary things, are undoubtedly anchored in Jewish messianism. The unique temporal idea, adapted from the religious sphere, which aspires to create a world- embracing humanity, that idea is now embodied in communism."[31] What was considered in 1889 to be a subversive revolutionary spirit, was now interpreted as the ideology of communism, which was perceived in Germany as the enemy of the people.

In his essay "The Jews and Modern Capitalism" (1911), the economist Werner Sombart proposed the theory of "Jewish revolutionism". This anti-semitic work depicts revolutionism as a Jewish activity, derived from the messianic idea. This activity, he writes, is destined "to deteriorate into unrest...for the Jew is always on the move, and cares not if he is a burden to those who wish for peace."[32] What was referred to in Catholic literature as "agitating and unquiet" is attributed by Sombart to the strong connection between money and Jewish mobility. The Jew has become "the master of Mammon" by means of which he aspires to "dominate the world", since money combines the two components of the Jewish spirit: "Saharism" and "nomadism". Money is not real like the country of origin of the Jews. Money is merely bulk "it is mobile....The constant concern of the Jews with money has diverted their attention from the natural, qualitative aspect of life, to the abstract and quantitative approach...They have become the masters of Mammon, and through it...the masters of the world."

The messianic hope, which throughout history instilled in the Jews an apocalyptic spirit of belief in a better future, was reduced by Sombart and many like-minded thinkers, into a 'teleological spirit'. As he wrote: "His view will be teleological, or a kind of practical rationalism...it is considered un-Jewish to live your life without having any aim...for the Jew, the entire universe is something created according to some plan." His conclusion is that the Jew is characterized by purposefulness, (as he calls it 'tachlis') which becomes his plan of action and policy.[33] Like Max Weber, Sombart assumed that the religion of a nation or a group had far-reaching influence on its economic life. Hence, he believed there to be an inherent connection between the Jewish religion and materialistic purposefulness and the international capitalist rule of the Jews. This conceptual linkage emptied Jewish messianism of its original religious significance, and imposed on Judaism the image of a utilitarian, exploitive outlook, with destructive impact on economic life and on modern life in general.[34] Through denying Jewish messianism Catholics came to believe that the Jewish religion had ceased to be a true religion.[35] It had been replaced by the new Christian faith, for "the era of the Old Testament had reached its end."[36] The Jewish people had forfeited their birthright and no longer had a mission to fulfil among other nations. Consequently, the denial of the Jews as God's chosen people, and rejection of their tradition were central themes of sermons.

The message of the fall of Israel, as delivered by preachers, was almost uniform in pattern, being divided into three parts: a) the sins of the Jews. b) the loss of their status as the chosen people. c) the triumph and superiority of Christianity. The sin, considered a grave one, was their denial of the messianism of Jesus. The intransigeance of the Jews had deprived them of the hope of salvation.[38] They were described as the eternal haters of Christ.[39] The image of the sinning and stubborn Jew, now dependent on the compassion of Jesus[40] was rooted in Christian by public consciousness, and the term 'heretic' was naturally attached to the word 'Jew'.[41] The Jewish heretics had rejected Jesus as messiah and saviour of the world, and what was the outcome? They in their turn were rejected by God.[42] Over and over again, the preachers told their audiences that the Jews had been "deprived of their birthright...which has been handed over to Catholics for now we are the chosen people."[43]

According to the Catholic version which was widely accepted, all the afflictions visited on the Jews were predetermined in the Divine scheme, which the prophets had foretold In order to give symbolic expression to the transfer of this birthright from "the children of the flesh to the children of the promise" (Romans 9,8), the materialist element in the appearance of the Jew was emphasized, and reference was made to "the Jew as flesh (fleischgesinnt) whose only interest is in earthly matters (auf das Irdische bezogen).[44] According to the Catholic catechism, the sacrifice of Isaac had bestowed on

Abraham the right to be called "father of the redeemer of the world," but this privilege was soon confined to the flesh" (dem Fleische nach).[45]

These views were filtered into the minds of the untutored masses in high-flown yet relatively simple terms. A single example from homiletic literature will illustrate this: the mission of the Jewish people was compared to the scaffolding supporting a house under construction. Once the building is completed, the scaffolding must be removed because, otherwise, it becomes a "troublesome and useless hindrance (unnuetziges und laestiges Hindernis). The Jews, in their efforts to preserve the scaffolding, have ignored the building. Therefore, nothing remains to them but the bitter task "of dragging to all corners of the earth the corpse of their religion" (Leichnam ihrer Religion) which is now of no value. Again, the answer to the inevitable question is given in clearly understandable language: Why preserve an abomination? Or in allegorical fashion: Why not rid themselves of the corpse? The answer rounds off the threefold theory of the "sin of the Jews -loss of their birthright- triumph of Christianity' by declaring that "the Jew must serve as perpetual testimony to Christianity".[46] And indeed, at almost every assembly, in every sermon, in every written edict dealing with Jews, the image of the eternal humiliation of Judaism as witness to the triumph of Christianity is reiterated. A popular manual of instruction for schools and churches, describes the exiling of the Jewish people in such a way as to suggest that it demonstrates the verity of the Catholic dogma. "We must recognize an additional intention of the Divine Providence, which is expressed in the Old Testament...It has given us a witness to substantiate the truth...the sworn enemy of Christianity, the entire Jewish people, can find in the Holy Scriptures - in which we believe- the verdict of its own eradication. Indeed, they had special reason and justification to root out these writings. Yet, nonetheless, they love this book as the most precious heritage of the religion of their forefathers. Wherever they are banished, they carry these books with them as the holiest of holies, and disseminate them among gentile nations. God did not wish this people, which deserved to be obliterated more than any other nation, to be entirely destroyed (gaenzlich ausgerottet), and this is so that we could have living proof of the truth of our sacred religion."[47]

To sum up: the loss of the birthright meant the invalidation of the eternal spiritual mission. Christian ideology relegated Israel to a temporal, transitory role. This being so, the Jews were not considered a spiritual force. Sermons emphasized their transience: the life span of the temporal is brief and it is destined to disappear. "The people of the synagogue....yearn only for worldly goods and for fleeting objects. Not so the church, which despises the material, and whose eyes are raised aloft to the celestial and the eternal."[48] Jesus was depicted by preachers as the antithesis of all temporal and fleshly things. His poverty was described as the ideal of asceticism and spirituality. "His kingdom has nothing in common with earthly wealth".[49] The Jews symbolize worldly riches and are seen by the church to find their happiness in materialism. They believe that the messiah will appear as a powerful and wealthy king who cannot be overpowered, and not as a modest, submissive and humble figure like Christ. The Jews refused to acknowledge the poor and humble man as their messiah, and hence they crucified him.[50]

The Catholic masses in towns and villages were given the historic opportunity to attribute to the "sinning nature" of the Jew all their everyday problems, failures and omissions, their financial distress, their problems of livelihood - for all these, their Jewish neighbour was to blame, since his evil and heretic spirit had disrupted their lives. Proof of the corruption of the Jew was now sought in the act of crucifixion. The priests presented the crucifixion as a historical event and not as an abstract lesson in Christian theology. It was a personal symbol for both ides: the crucifying Jew as the Personification of evil and the crucified Jesus as the embodiment of good.

The charge of deicide (Gottesmord) widened the gap between Jew and Christian. "The greatest crime ever committed under the sun, is undoubtedly deicide."[51] "The most abominable of all crimes" was committed by the Jews as revenge against Jesus. For, in this people" in these enraged people all human feeling is apparently dead," and hence "we Christians despise them."[52] "The deicide committed by the Jews exceeds in its evil all other crimes," "a despicable and horrifying act" (graessliche Untat).[53] And as the inflammatory sermon reached its height, a prayer was recited calling for "the annihilation of these impudent desecrators of Divine law."[54]

"Criminal hands" were raised against the saviour, the hands of "cunning serpents who inflict their poisonous bite from a secret place."[55]

One need only examine a list of the terms and epithets used by the preachers to understand how their audiences perceived the Jews: murderers, criminals, evil ones, sinners, enraged, inhuman, despicable, corrupt, desecrators, impudent, cunning serpents, poisonous, enemies of God. These words were not directed at individual Jews, but at the entire Jewish people: "They, once the preferred among all nations, have now become garbage, and in this miserable conditions they live to this very day."[56] "The sworn enemy of Christianity is the *entire Jewish people* (italics mine Z.B.), and the evidence of their rejection by God may be found in the Scriptures."[57]

NOTES

1.   Rosenzweig, p. 362.

2.   Thoma, p. 17.

3.   Rosenzweig. See also translator's note, p. 363.

4.   Pattis, p. 635.

5.   Kroenes, p. 143.

6.   Flusser, in Thoma, p. 25f, 29 and in Flusser's Jesus, p. 10.

7.   Kotte, p. 147.

8.   Gradaus, p. 31.

9.   Moore, p. 18: "The liberation of the Jews is a loss for Judaism and not for Christianity...We will liberate them from ancient slavery, from their situation, and from their hatred of Christianity."

10.   Kroenes, Vol 7, 1859, p. 444.

11.   Gradaus, p. 76.

12.   Philothea, Yearbook 15, No. 50, 1851, p. 394.

13.   Saffenreuther, Part 1, 1840, p. 18.

14.   Zollner, Yearbook 2, Vol 1, 1869, p. 386.

15.   Gretsch, Vol 3, 1882, p. 40.

16.   Kroenes, Vol 3, 1856, p. 47.

17.   Flusser, Jesus, p. 28, 36, 102 and Thoma, pp. 87-95.

18.   Endler, p. 131.

19.   Hammerstein, p. 193.

20.   Katholik, Vol 86, 1842, p. 160.

21.   Lexikon..., p. 629.

22.   Hungari, p. 345.

62

23.   Cohen, p. 260, as follows: "Although the Protocols were an important part of one of the main totalitarian beliefs of the twentieth century, they grew up out of an ancient apocalyptic tradition. The extent to which they were linked from the outset to the legend of the Antichrist is clearly implicit in the comment which Sergei Nilos added to his 1905 edition, as translated in the first British edition of the Protocols (1920)."

24.   Historische-Politische Blaetter, Vol. 22, 1848, p. 618.   On the Antichrist, see below, Chapter 8.

24a.   See below p. 18.

25.   Hungari, p. 345; and also Heim, p. 116.

26.   See, for example, the (anonymous) lampoon "Der Mauschel-Jude".

27.   Among the various lexicons was Wetzer Staatslexikon, third edition, 1909; fifth edition, 1927.

28.   Wetzer, Vol. 6, p. 1937.

29.   Christlich-Soziale Blaetter, 1878, pp. 234-237; "The revolutionary status of Judaism."

30.   Staatslexikon, 1909, p. 1470.

31.   Staatslexikon, 1927, p. 1650.

32.   Sombart, p. 251; and see *ibid.*, also critical foreword by B. Hoselitz.

33.   *Ibid.*, p. 249, 250.

34.   *Ibid.*, p. 323.

35.   Ehrler, p. 392; Diessel, p. 622.

36.   Faulhaber, p. 194.

37.   Kroenes, Vol., p. 143.

38.   Patiss, p. 267.

39.   Schmuelling, p. 486.

40.   Lettan, p. 5.

41.   Kroenes, Vol. 12, 1862, p. 143.

42.   Fuhlrott, p. 24; Siebert, p. 41; Schmuelling, p. 48; Patiss, p. 635; Heim, Vol. 3, p. 55.

43.   Fuhlrott, p. 27.

44.   Colmar, p. 140.

45.   Mehler, p. 117; "and notwithstanding, Abraham, through his only son Isaac, became the father of the entire Jewish people, and the fleshy father of the Divine redeemer..."

46.   Segur, p. 61n.

47.   Deharbe/1, Vol. IV, 1869, p. 150.

48.   Kroenes, Vol. 8, 1859, p. 362.

49.   Gradaus, p. 70.

50.   Ventura, p. 394; Nickel, p. 61; Gradaus, p. 61.

51.   Ventura, p. 148; Diessel, p. 250.

52.   Gradaus, p. 100, 200.

53.   Deharbe/2, p. 389; Schmuelling, p. 1.

54.   Colmar, p. 152.

55.   Patiss, p. 267, 696.

56.   Hungari, p. 168.

57.   Deharbe/1, Vol. 4, 1869, p. 150. And see also study by Bishop, p. 22; "The allegation that Jesus was rejected by all his people is flatly contradicted by the Gospels. A French-language annual used in Switzerland attempts to shift the responsibility of Jesus' death to the Jewish leaders, but at the same time charges the whole people with rejecting him."

CHAPTER EIGHT

THE INHUMAN JEW: THE ANTICHRIST, THE ETERNAL JEW, THE PHARISEE

An additional anti-Christian characteristic was attributed to the Jews. Because of their rejection of Christ, the Messiah, they were identified with the Antichrist. Under "Antichrist', Kroenes' popular lexicon stated that according to the church fathers, the Antichrist had originated among the Jews, in the tribe of Dan (Jeremiah 8,16). He would conquer the Land of Israel and establish his dwelling place in Jerusalem.[1] The common feature of the Antichrist and the eternal Jew (see below), was the fact that they were not mortal. The Antichrist, through his demonic power, and the eternal Jew, who is unable to die, symbolize the everlasting, supernatural powers of darkness. The identification of the Antichrist with the Jew is an example of the discrepancy between theological theories and popular incitement against the Jews. The *Historische Blaetter* were inspired by Catholic interests and the anti-Jewish incitement was influenced by current events and the Zeitgeist. The arbitrary and tendentious use of these images had no roots in official theological views. Theological literature claimed that there was no consensus among the church fathers as to the identity of the Antichrist. Even if there was accord on certain points, this was not the official, binding view of the church. The Antichrist was sometimes a specific Jew, but was also identified with the Jewish people as a whole or, according to one view, with Satan. Others identified him with Nero and another source broached the theory that he was the universal personification of anti-Christian forces. Our discussion is concerned, not with theological viewpoints as such, but with their popularization by the masses and the public at large. They were not swayed by speculative interpretations. To them, it was indisputably clear that the Jew was the Antichrist.

The term 'Antichrist' enfolds two meanings, the first universal and the second individual and personal. Two essences are inherent in Jesus: the divine insofar as he is God, and the earthly, when he takes human form. Both meanings had considerable influence on forging the negative image of the Jew. In the personal sense, this term implied resistance to the man Christ, to his deeds and ideas. The antagonism towards Christ as a human being took on historical significance, and the term Antichrist aroused human and temporal associations. He was perceived as the enemy of this world. In the universal sense, the Antichrist was taken to symbolize the demonic and diabolical elements, the satanic forces struggling against God. The combination of the two meanings summoned up in the Christian imagination a monstrous image of the Jew. As an anti-historical, anti-human force, his very existence was the embodiment of evil. In this spirit it was written that "although God hates wickedness...both sacred and profane history have raised monsters among the human race whose mission is to serve as a warning to all nations...Isaiah described the Jews as a wicked people."[2] The wickedness of the Jewish people should serve as a warning to Christians: they should learn "from the Jew what not to be" (wie du nicht seyn sollst). He also personified the reverse of Divine good "as implementor of the will of Hell and as Satan's evildoer, he murdered the Messiah."[3] The characterization of the Jew as Antichrist took on substance and found its tangible expression in the description of the 'eternal Jew', who was identified by Christian exegesis with Ahasueras. The Christian legend of the wandering Jew apparently evolved from the interpretation given to in the story of the arrest of Jesus on the road to Golgotha: "And when he had thus spoken, one of the officers which stood by struck Jesus with the palm of his hand, saying 'Answerest thou the high priest so?' (John 18,22) According to the legend, the blow was struck by a Jerusalem cobbler named Ahasueras. Over the centuries the legend gathered momentum, until Ahasueras was identified with the entire Jewish people.[4] The wanderings and sufferings of the Jewish people now came to serve as the symbol of their culpability for the crucifixion, which will last until Jesus appears once more on earth (Matthew 15,28; John 21,20-22).

The image of the eternally wandering Jew was a major theme in sermons. Some preachers referred directly to Ahasueras, but the sin and guilt were usually attributed to the entire Jewish people, condemned to wander and to be scattered among the nations. To quote from one of these sermons: "Ahasueras rejects Jesus. From that moment, Ahasueras wanders as a refugee, like another Cain. He seeks tranquillity and does not find it. He must live without respite, without rest, tortured and humiliated - the eternal Jew...*This is not historical truth* (Italics mine Z.B.) but the meaning is profound. Ahasueras is the symbol of the Jewish people who rejected their messiah. He symbolizes any man who rejects Jesus...his enemy is Christ's cross....he is still the eternal Jew throughout the world."[5] It is interesting to note the comment that this is not historical truth but that the meaning is profound. This is one of the characteristic indications of prejudice in general and of hatred of Jews in particular. Prejudices are not adopted as a result of research and examination but through a priori value judgment, which is detached from historical truth. This calls to mind an apt parallel, (even though the comparison may appear startling). When Hitler referred to the 'Protocols of the Elders of Zion', he declared that it was immaterial to him whether the text corresponded to historical truth. Even if it was at odds with the truth "the inner truth inherent in it is more persuasive".[6] The profound meaning sought in the legend of the wandering Jew, the inner truth ostensibly inherent in the Protocols, are among the deeply-entrenched foundations of anti-semitism. The revilers of the Jews and of Judaism are not interested in examining the veracity of their claims. For them, the a priori goal is the prime factor, and the end justifies the means, even at the expense of historical truth.

The image of the wandering Jew has an additional dimension. To wander without a defined destination is an indication of impotence and ineffectuality. It implies that the end of the road is at hand, or, as a Catholic theologian wrote, it writes off the history of the Jewish people, and all that remains is Ahasueras wandering aimlessly throughout the world.[7] A nation

68

which lacks history, is a hazard to mankind, but according to the Catholic catechism. Providence wanted the Jewish people to remain on earth in order to bear witness to the truth of the Christian creed.[8]

Sermons highlighted the inner connection between Cain, Ahasueras and the Jewish people. The link was the curse weighing on all of them.

The mark of Cain rests on the Jew in whom is fulfilled the curse "A fugitive and a vagabond shalt thou be" and "the Lord set a mark on him."[9] Thus, the wandering Jew is "another Cain".[10] Sermons created a fictitious analogy between the fate of Cain and of the Jewish people. The audience absorbed the message - which they perceived as a historical fact - that a divine curse rested on the Jewish people.

Another, central theme in Catholic literature and sermons, was the fate of the city of Jerusalem. It was sacred to the two religions, Christianity and Judaism. To Judaism - because it was the site of the Temple, to Christianity - because of the life, death and hoped-for resurrection of Jesus, linked by tradition to Jerusalem. In other words: Jerusalem was the city of the once-chosen people, and the city of the crucifixion of God's chosen heir. The flowering of the Jewish city meant the decline of Christianity, while the ruined Jerusalem was testimony to the triumph of Christianity. Because of this contradiction, and because "ancient Jerusalem was the capital and center of Judaism, Jesus wished to die in that city."[11]

As noted, the death of Christ was attributed to the grave historical sin of the Jews, and the retribution for their crime was the destruction of Jerusalem, the annulling of their status as chosen people and their dispersal to the four corners of the earth. In other words, the destruction of Jerusalem was dependent on the crucifixion of Jesus, the greatest sin the Jews had committed. The crucifixion was seen as the divine sign of the fall of the city. Jesus, said the preachers "distanced himself from the Jews, abandoned the Temple of the Old Testament, in order to enter into the halls of the New Testament."[12]

The revoking of the status of chosen people, and conferring of this honour on a new entity, was perceived as a miracle which occurred in Jerusalem. When Jesus was crucified "the miracle occurred. The curtain of the Holy of Holies was torn. All this came to show, no less than the casting away of the Jews from God...that their prayer and their divine worship had been annulled: their Temple was abandoned to ruins and they ceased to be the people of God."[13] The destruction of the Temple and of Jerusalem were described in gloomy and sharp images, and the preachers usually identified good with the victor and evil with the vanquished Jews. Jerusalem was no longer an important city, it no longer belongs to the Jews. "God punished the chosen people since they did not acknowledge the Saviour."[14]

Churchgoers were told that after the city was destroyed, many Jews stole outside the walls under cover of darkness, but were caught, tortured and crucified. And this, "dear Christians, was fitting punishment, for they had caught the son of God, tortured and crucified him."[15]

The idea of sin and punishment, with emphasis on the moral superiority of the inflicter of punishment, is given popular form, in line with tradition, so as to convey a tangible and vivid message to the simple masses.[16] One of the manuals of instruction for the catechist and the Christian family describes the destruction of Jerusalem. According to the narrative, a Jewish woman of distinguished family (*vornehme*) named Mary lived there. Because of the appalling conditions in the city, she suffered starvation, and therefore "slaughtered her child and cooked him in order to satisfy her hunger; a terrible deed, how unlike that of the other Mary, who stood under the cross of her son..."[17] The author based this tale on the story told in the Book of Lamentations (4,10), which contains an allegorical description of mothers in Jerusalem who fed on their children. The misrepresentation is blatant: an allegory is treated as a true event. One may assume that such a story had a strong impact on its listeners, and helped the preacher make his point. The curse on Jerusalem has been retained in the Catholic catechism to the present day. Today as well, we find similar expressions, used covertly or openly.[18]

Several of the church fathers claimed that the Antichrist originated among the Jews, and that his dwelling place was Jerusalem. The credulous audience of the preachers received a totally negative picture of the Jew who had murdered Christ, and believed him to be the Antichrist whose sin had brought down upon him the destruction of Jerusalem. The ultimate image may be summarized in one word: *Unmensch*, or inhuman creature.[19] And now let us examine another aspect of the Jewish image.

The Catholic catechism did not spare the Pharisees. Judaism, as a real, albeit negative historical phenomenon - rather than an anti-Christian idea - was identified with the Pharisees. The term 'Pharisaism' (Pharisaeertum) was invented, to describe a creed marked by corruption and hypocrisy, and it became a synonym for the hated Jews. Hence, it is not surprising that this sect came under considerable attack in Catholic literature and sermons. It is easy to guess why the Pharisees were chosen as the symbol of Judaism. In 70 CE, after the destruction of the Temple, a great social upheaval occurred among the Jews. The Saduccees ceased, in effect, to exist as a class and sect, while the Pharisees became the acknowledged leaders of the people, and as such, their spokesmen in the confrontation with Christianity.[20]

The doctrines and practices of the Pharisees are beyond the scope of the present study. It is relevant, however, to examine the subject in the context of the Catholic catechism, in order to comprehend the methods adopted in the war on Judaism. The Pharisee-Jew connection was rooted planted in the minds of Christians, as a result of Catholic indoctrination.[21] Several quotations from Catholic homiletic literature can serve to illustrate the method.

The Pharisees are presented as the enemies of Jesus, motivated by two instincts: hatred and envy.[22] "Their envy consumed them for they saw Jesus was beloved by the people; his modesty and humility shamed them. Why was Jesus obliged to suffer because the wicked men could not tolerate the holy God and the reign of justice in this world."[23]

One of the sermons, in a collection of one hundred and twenty sermons for children, expounds two central motifs: the Pharisees as the foes of Jesus and the symbol of evil. They were described as 'base heretics' (*niedertraechtige Verleumder*) with only one aim, "to vilify the deeds and words of the divine saviour."[24]

For the Christian, the Pharisee symbolized hypocrisy, arrogance and contempt for others[25] and Pharisaism was considered to be synonymous with religious hypocrisy (Religioese Luege). These aspersions were supported by quotations from the New Testament (Matthew 5, 20).[26]

The Pharisees were denounced as hypocrites "and this is indeed the most suitable epithet for people who uttered the name of God but bear Satan in their hearts...even today there are Christian Pharisees in great numbers who conceal their bottomless wickedness...History, with its cautionary examples, leads us to recognize the wicked actions of these hypocrites."[27] The author of the sermon listed a number of historical figures who were guilty of 'Pharisaism': 'the hypocritical Cain,' the greatest of hypocrites; 'Herod', murderer of the children from Bethlehem, until he reached 'the most contemptible of all, Judas, betrayer of God." (The identification of Judah Iscariot with the entire Jewish people has endured to the present day).[28] Pharisaism was pictured as a warning and a frightening example (abschreckendes warnendes Beispiel) for all those guilty of the sin of excessive self-confidence, which leads a man to stoicism.[29] The author of the Apologie des Christenthums, considers Pharisaism to be close in spirit (Geistesverwandten) to Greek stoicism, but adds cynically that Pharisees "at least pretend to be righteous men through their external actions."[30] The same author described everyday life in ancient Rome as 'Pharisaism', in order to illustrate the hypocrisy which prevailed in that society. In order to exemplify the hypocritical and immoral conduct of Cato the elder towards women, he accused him of 'Pharisaism'.[31]

The combination of 'pharisaic' traits and human failings, added another dimension to the negative image of the Jew. Priests could now point to actual historical figures, who personified the 'worship of the letter of the law' and 'rigid legalism', lack of inspiration, narrow-mindedness, a hypocritical approach to observance of the law. The Pharisees "display contempt for the important religious precepts given by God", they "observe meticulously only external matters (Aussendinge)."[32] The justice to which they aspired was "a matter of outward show....but within they are sanctimonious and wicked."[33] "They discussed and debated religious matters every day, but without true faith."[34] In modern times, Pharisaical traits have been interpreted as the corruption of 'the true religious spirit'.[35]

72

The preachers delivered these inflammatory statements in blunt and simple language, adapted to the capacity for understanding of their flock.[36] Having examined several of the central themes of the sermons which helped to establish the negative image of the Jew, we can sum up the methods utilized by the preachers in the following diagram. One can distinguish two stages with internal classifications:

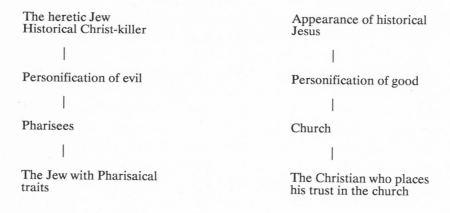

THE CELESTIAL STAGE GUIDING PROVIDENCE
|
THE EARTHLY-HISTORICAL STAGE

The heretic Jew Historical Christ-killer	Appearance of historical Jesus
|	|
Personification of evil	Personification of good
|	|
Pharisees	Church
|	|
The Jew with Pharisaical traits	The Christian who places his trust in the church

The method appears relatively simple. In order to preserve schematic simplicity, detailed discussion was avoided with regard to the heavenly sphere. The focus on Jesus as an actual historical figure, i.e. the move down to the second stage, made it easier for the clergy to put across their message. With regard to Jesus, mankind was divided into the heretic Jews and the Christian believers. However, the concepts of personification of good and personification of evil were abstract, and were therefore translated into the language of historical fact. Good became the church, evil became the Pharisees.

NOTES

1.   Kroenes, Vol I, 1856, pp. 312/3 13; Knoll, p. 363; Scherer, p. 105. On the Antichrist in theological exegesis, see: Wetzer, I, 1882, pp. 917-926 and particularly p. 923; and the summary in modern literature: Lexikon Theologie, 1, pp. 634-638; and see Norman Cohen, p. 52.

2.   Kroenes, Vol 2. 1856, p. 388.

3.   Saffenreuther, p. 186; Schmuelling, p. 391.

4.   Neubauer; Liefman, E., pp. 122-156 neither the statement on the Antichrist nor on Ahasueras were originally anti-semitic in intent. These undertones were added only under contemporary influences. The image of Ahasueras gradually lost its tragic implications, and, as in the case of the legend of the Antichrist, crude jokes and anti-semitic allusions were connected with it. Towards the end of the 18th century, Ahasueras became the subject of a popular game. Liefman, p. 147.

5.   Frommel, p. 213.

6.   Rauschning, p. 235.

7.   Klug, p. 44.

8.   Deharbe/l, Vol. 4, 1869, p. 150; Gradaus, p. 27; Gretsch, p. 71.

9.   Scherer, p. 15.

10.   Frommel, p. 213.

11.   Martin, p. 13.

12.   Saffenreuther, p. 173.

13.   Hungari, *op. cit.*, sermon of Weiser, p. 167.

14.   Gradaus, Vol 3, 1861, p. 170.

15.   Saffenreuther, p. 461.

16.   On the method used in the sermons, see below.

17.   Rolfus, p. 123, and see Ecclesiasticus 4,10.

18.   Bishop, p. 1:   "Thus was the prophesy of Jesus Christ (Spanish textbook, p. 19) against Jerusalem fulfilled. A terrible punishment for the sin of deicide." (PD 113,12).

"Siege of Jerusalem - soon the Deicide city would suffer the punishment foretold by Jesus Christ himself. A punishment unique in the history of peoples." (PD 114, 13).

"This Jerusalem, the Chosen City which (French textbook, p. 20) would not recognize the One who came to her in the Lord's name, will be rejected." (L 145,8,82).

"Earthly Jerusalem had fulfilled her mission; soon she could be blotted out." (L 263,24,123).

19.   Knoll, p. 287.

20.   Eschelbacher, p. 78; in homiletic literature, the Pharisees are described as the leaders of the people. See: Knoll, p. 128; Koerber, p. 27.

21.   Bishop, p. 55:

"To explore more fully the mindset resulting from religious teaching, respondents were given the parable of the Pharisee and the tax collector (Luke, 18:10-14) to read; they were then asked to state which one was typically Jewish and to explain in their own words why." (LB,1 14).

"One quarter (23% students, 26% adults) thought the Pharisee was typically Jewish in a negative sense, because he was conceited' or 'hypocritical' or 'sectarian minded'. As the Louvain report states: "an identification will be created between these different concepts encompassing within the same reality the Jews in Jesus' time, the Pharisees and present-day Jews." (*ibid.*, p. 22).

22.   On the Pharisees in Christian exegesis, see Flusser, Jesus, pp. 5off; and Thoma, pp. 175ff, 219ff.

23.   Frank, p. 289; Kroenes, Vol 9, p. 272.

24.   *Ibid.*, Vol 12, 1862, p. 307.

25.   *Ibid.*, Vol 6, 1858, p. 201; Schmidt, Vol 2, p. 539.

26.   Wenzel, p. 24; Kroenes, Vol 6, 1858, p. 201: "Faith: The Pharisees are an example of false faith. It is marked by pride, self-importance. The Pharisee prays to himself and boasts of his worship. His thoughts are centered on himself and not on his Creator, and like all seeming believers, they despise others and boast of their own deeds..."

27.   Wolfgarten, p. 570.

28.   *Ibid.*, p. 573. On p. 572 it is stated: "And thus we set before our eyes some of the hypocritical figures from the Bible, in order to recognize who were those rejected people, who are thus even today. " See also Bishop, p. 34:

(French example): "God's enemies were the Jews themselves. A mystery of wickedness hardened their hearts. All human perversity concentrated itself and culminated in the hearts of the Pharisees of Judea."(L, 130,49:96).

29.   Modern research cites the critical view of a Catholic priest named Teske, which we quote here in translation. See: Eckert, p. 217: "The image of the traitor certainly had a negative impact on the evaluation of the Jews. The similar ring of the name easily led to identification of the Jews with Judah -'such are the Jews'. In this context, particular attention should be paid to the Pharisees, for Jesus' harsh words against the Pharisees were diverted to apply to the Jews in general. Every chapter of the gospels which dealt with the Pharisees generated a strongly negative attitude towards the Jews."

Stoicism: a Graeco-Roman school of philosophy which advocated a materialist outlook, namely that the laws of nature and of the conscience direct human life. Divinity was perceived as an active rational cause, and hence, the entire universe was perceived as an entity directed by rational law. For the stoic, a good man is a wide man. His wisdom is evident in his conduct of his life according to the laws of nature.

30.   Weiss, p. 116.

31.   *Ibid.*, pp. 421, 422.

32.   Deharbe/2, p. 48.

33.   Melchers, p. 124.

34.   Heim, Vol 3, 1839, p. 55.

35.   The modern New Catholic Encyclopaedia explains the term Pharisee obliquely. *Ibid.*, Vol XI, p. 252:

"They offered various opinions on minute observance of these and other precepts degenerating into rigorism and casuistry. The result was frequently a sterile externalism destructive of a real spirit...Later rabbinical schools looked back in admiration upon the Pharisees as the true upholders of Israel's law and tradition."

36.   See above, pp. 26-28.

CHAPTER NINE

THE KULTURKAMPF AGAINST THE MODERN JEW

The image of the Jew, as formulated in the Catholic (and Protestant) camps, was assimilated into Christian consciousness in the course of history. In this process, the Christian-theological view, which identified in the Jewish character traits of formalism and narrow-minded legalism, was increasingly supplanted. What the priests had denoted 'biblical materialism' was transmuted among the various anti-Jewish trends into 'social materialism'. The practical observance of biblical injunctions was interpreted as pragmatism, as an indication of materialistic nature obsessed with petty concerns, with material objects or, as modern accusers claim - money for its own sake. According to a manual for catechistic instruction: "If skill in conducting financial affairs were a recommendation for the essence of a religion, which religion would then be considered the best? Apparently, Judaism."[1]

Historically speaking, the transition from theological anti-Judaism to personal, socio-political hatred of Jews, occurred not in the nineteenth century, but earlier. However, we are not concerned with this historical development.[2] But rather with examining the attitude towards the Jews, on the basis of Catholic pronouncements throughout Germany, in order to ascertain to what extent there was a transition from theological to socio-political arguments. The theme of exile as expounded in sermons and homiletic literature can serve as historical evidence that the Jews, dispersed throughout the world, were considered to be agitating elements in their surroundings. The biblical Jew belonged to the religious faith of the past, and the view of this historical image depended to no small extent on the rhetorical skills of the preacher. The wandering Jew is no longer identified with the legendary Ahasueras, but has now become a flesh-and-blood contemporary of the modern Christians and ever present among them. And this presence recalled and symbolized the collective curse imposed on Jews.

Theological arguments were expounded in sermons and in homiletic literature, but they were obscured and even suppressed in light of the face-to-face encounter between the sides. It was the Jew, as seen in everyday life, who was the materialist, the money-grabber, the great enemy of Christianity in this world. An example of this view is the story about Rothschild related by a certain preacher. It contains no biblical allusions. The congregation were told of the great wealth of Baron Rothschild. A Christian, who had heard of Rothschild, met him in an inn and expressed the wish to see for himself "his great pile of money' (Grossen Geldhaufen). The Christian was even willing to pay for the Baron's consent. The preacher went on to quote Rothschild's answer as follows: "The Jew answered by saying, give me the coin and I will show you my pile of money." When the visitor stood amazed in Rothschild's apartment and asked him "How did you make all this money?" the Jew replied "By this method, I added to the pile coin by coin."[3]

The Catholic Apologetica mentioned above referred approvingly to the biblical precepts regarding marital life, education and respect for women. On the other hand, harsh things were said about the negative influence of modern Judaism on the patriotic sentiments of other nations.[4] The accusations now hurled at the Jews developed into overt anti-semitism in accord with the spirit of the times. James Parkes has noted the distinction between anti-Judaism and anti-semitism. In defining modern political anti-semitism, he wrote that this hatred was 'invented' to serve aims which had nothing to do with the Jewish people or the Jewish religion. And herein lies the true difference: the Christians, in light of their religion, believed in their imputations against the Jews. Modern anti-semitism, on the other hand, which seeks to free itself of all theological dogmas, although influenced by them - could manoeuvre its anti-Jewish theories and actions inconsistently. This ability attests to its political nature. However, both manifestations were anti-semitic, and hence one should not underestimate the anti-semitic character of theological anti-Judaism, whose origins were mainly sought in the New Testament. St. John, in his attack on 'the Jew' paved the way for all-encompassing hatred of the Jews.[5] In its modern social context, the traditional religious conflict served as indication of the class gap between Jew and Christian. This gap widened in modern times, and this fact was reflected in sermons. "In places where the Jews dwell among the Christian population, the Christians are poverty stricken, while the Jews suck their blood like vampires." And, again, it was stated that money rules the world, and hence the power of the Mammon Jews.[6] The assimilation of the Jews into their surroundings was intensive and was facilitated by their political and social emancipation. This emancipation, though never fully implemented, considerably expedited social, cultural and economic rapprochement between Jews and non-Jews.[7] The closer contact between them increased the value judgment - both negative and positive- concerning Jews. Negative views were reinforced, paradoxically enough, by advocates of equal rights for Jews. When Christian Wilhelm Dohm, in 1781, issued his appeal for equal civil rights for Jews, he spoke of the Verbesserung, the 'improvement' of the Jews, which suggests that he was starting out from a negative viewpoint of the Jewish way of life. Some hundred years later, in the eighteen eighties, when the 'Anti-semitic League' was set up in Germany, leaders of the Catholic Center Party, (founded after the establishment of the Reich by Bismarck), attacked the anti-semitic demands of the League. August Reichensperger[*] and Ludwig Windthorst[*] championed the cause of Jewish rights. But even this pro-Jewish stand did not stem from disinterested admiration. The Catholics constituted a minority in the German population, and as such could not permit the discrimination of another minority - such as the Jews - because of their concern for their own standing. There was a note of reservation, (reminiscent of Dohm) here as well: "Possibly this activity (of the League Z.B.) will produce useful results, that is to say, will teach the Jewish citizens who live among us, of the need to act with more consideration and moderation....the serious question always remains, namely, have the hopes pinned on the Emancipation really been realized..."[8] The pronouncements of the Catholic clergy in Germany created a paradoxical situation. The intensification of liberalization and modernist trends in German society, in which the Jews played an active role, might have been expected to mitigate anti-semitism; however, the reverse occurred. There was an upsurge of anti-Jewish activity. The spiritual succour which the priests offered in their sermons, with the aim of 'saving souls' from modernism, constituted the base for unrestrained attacks on the Jews, who were charged with being disseminators of liberalism and modernism. In the Kulturkampf between Catholicism and liberalism, between papal authority and secular-state power, which broke out in 1870, there were three components which affected the status and situation of the Jews of Germany.

a) The Catholics became a minority in the Reich, which was now mainly Protestant, since Schleswig Holstein, Hanover, Kurhessen, Nassau and Frankfurt were annexed to Protestant Prussia after 1866.

b) The founding of the Centre Party in 1870.

c) The victory of the Catholic side in the Kulturkampf.

From 1874, the Centre Party was the second largest party in the Reichstag. For the Jews, these above-mentioned components were highly significant. In times of crisis, the Catholics launched onslaughts on the Jews, since they regarded them as the liberal adversary, and identified them with the hated Protestant enemy. In times of triumph, they blamed the Jews for the Kulturkampf . The anti-Jewish tone was particularly aggressive at the beginning of the Kulturkampf, and drew its inspiration, inter alia, from the pronouncements of Pope Pius IX, who condemned the Jews for their avarice.[9] In the Herder Lexikon, which was to be found in many German homes, the modern anti-social element is clearly emphasized in the description of the Jew: "The scattered Jews no longer have a history." In the East, it was stated, they would suffer less, because "their oriental entity is suited to that place. There is no constant confrontation with Christianity, and their nomadic business spirit will not encounter the hostility of the sovereign nation." It was also said that "the religious fanaticism of the Christian nations during the Crusades exacerbated the persecution of the Jews, for they were seen as the descendants of the murderers of Christ....The Church took an emphatic stand against this atmosphere of persecution, but, on the other hand, it was the Jews themselves who, through their tendency to practice usury (Wuchergeist), contributed to their own persecution..."[10] A later edition of the same lexicon notes that "the Jews became a social force after they were granted concessions by modern legislation, and became the owners of big capital (Grosskapital), and of the large industrial concerns (Grossproduktion)..."[11]

The Kulturkampf greatly stimulated the growth of the Catholic press in Germany and expanded its circulation. In early 1872 there were 126 Catholic newspapers (for 15 million Catholics). In 1890, after the struggle ended, 298 papers circulated. Between 1871 and 1888, the Catholic press doubled its circulation, and reached 630,000 in 1881.[12] The main issue preoccupying the Catholics during their struggle with Bismarck was the Emancipation, namely the demand for "the emancipation of man in modern culture and modern society."[13] On the one hand, the Catholics demanded emancipation for themselves in the Protestant countries in which they constituted a minority, and considered the attainment of equal rights to be a vital need. On the other hand, they condemned emancipation as such as a modern and liberal historical phenomenon with the potential to destroy the theological and ecclesiastical order. It was regarded as a process of abandonment of Catholic tradition, and the representative of that secular modernism which was undermining the foundations of the church. Confronted with Bismarck's hostility towards Catholics, they identified the forces of anti-Catholicism, emancipation and modernism with Protestantism and Judaism. In the fervour of this debate, theological arguments were introduced into the socio-political attacks. The insubstantiality of the religious issue here, can be ascertained from the anti-semitic essay written by Wilhelm Marr.[14] While a Christian, he considered himself neither a Protestant nor Catholic, nor member of any socialist movement, but as a bystander, member of the German *national* elite which aspired to leadership of the Reich.[15] In his article, 'Der Sieg des Judenthums uber das Germanenthum', he declared: "With the spread of Christianity in the West, there emerged an ostensibly religious hatred of Jews. The folly of the religious aspects of this hatred is already manifest in the attempt to blame the Jews for the crucifixion of Christ - a deed known to have been committed by the Roman authorities in response to the demands of the cowardly

Jerusalem mob. That same Jewish mob in the time of Christ did nothing but what has always been done by mobs, in all eras and among all nations....and if indeed, there were fanatic Jews in the Middle Ages who 'slaughtered Christian children' for the festival of Passover....if there were indeed such insane happenings,- and there is no historical evidence of this,- these were crimes like any others, and do not justify universal religious hatred....I therefore offer my protection to the Jews against any 'religious' persecution.[16] Marr, who was officially a Protestant, is significant for our discussion, since he did not adopt a religious standpoint in censuring the Jews, and hence his arguments fit in with the Catholic attack on the Jews as possessors of destructive, liberal and modern power, which incites anti-Catholic forces to action.

Prominent among the popular Catholic periodicals of the time were the Historische-Politische Blaetter. It was claimed there that the Kulturkampf could not have taken place without the Jews, since it was of supreme political advantage for them, achieving directly what money could have achieved only obliquely. The struggle enabled them - borne aloft on the wave of Protestant fanaticism and liberal zeal - to rise to the status of a ruling partner.[17] Another Catholic periodical wrote disapprovingly of the reciprocal influence of Protestantism and the Jewish spirit. Protestant rationalism, it said, had become the accomplice of the Jewish spirit which is doing excellent business with the 'Enlightenment swindle' (Humanitätsschwindel) just as it succeeds in 'stock-exchange deals.'[18]

Liberalism and control of capital were presented to unsophisticated Christians as anti-Catholic, Jewish manifestations: "Wherever people deny Jesus and worship money, there, by natural right, the Jews take control."[19] Liberalism was being disseminated by the triumphant Jews, who were penetrating into the heart of Christian Europe, for example into the British parliament "where the prospect of great business deals has been opened up for Semitism, but Christian England will rapidly forfeit its character and firm position.... this is the beginning of a process of emptying of the content of Christianity in England (Entchristlichung)."[20] Wrathful Catholics denounced Jewish influence as "new paganism", and described "Macchiavelli and the Jew Spinoza" as "the true prophets of the revolutionary century."[21]

In the course of the nineteenth century, Catholic writings drew a distinction between traditional Judaism, strictly observing all the religious laws, and modern emancipated Judaism, striving to liberate itself from the yoke of religion.   This distinction emerged against the background of contemporary changes. In mid-century, the process of civil integration of the Jews in Gentile society came to fruition, and "the Jews moved over from their previous patterns of life which were specifically Jewish, to what was accepted in their non-Jewish surroundings."[22] This integration was accompanied by secularization processes, as some Jews regarded the existence of the Jewish framework as an obstacle to full emancipation. This rationalist secular approach was attacked by Catholic circles, which identified it with the Protestant spirit.[23]   Rationalism, it was explained, was the outcome of "abandonment of the Talmud" by "young Israel" who had renounced "the divine sanctity of the teachings of Moses". Such modern Jews lacked national pride, and were characterized, in their new milieu, by "national fury" (Nationalingrimm) against Christian society.[24]   In these attacks it is interesting to note the drastic change in attitude. The Talmud and Jewish halakha, which were once the objects of virulent attacks, were now perceived as positive features of the traditional Jewish lifestyle.   It should be understood, however, that this change was merely a tactical move on the part of Catholics, who were anxious to appear both tolerant and liberal, in line with the mood of the times. Catholicism, which gained political strength after the Kulturkampf, sought to appear progressive, and to cancel the impression that it was a weak and backward class, as had been the case before. Since the demand for civil rights presupposed a certain degree of tolerance, the Catholics adopted this stand towards traditional Judaism. By distinguishing between the modern and the traditional, they maintained their facade of tolerance, on the one hand, and were able more easily to direct their onslaughts against the modern, anti-traditional Jew, on the other. Thus, observance of the religious precepts and respect for the Talmud were considered manifestations of institutionalized, traditional and true Judaism, while the attraction to modernist trends was interpreted as Protestant heresy, the fruit of Jewish influences. Catholic "tolerance" was displayed only

84

towards the traditional Jew who had not been tempted by the lure of modernism.[25]

An example of this Catholic tactic can be found in an article published in the Catholic periodical, *Hochland*, dealing with Jewish marital relations and family hygiene.. Though the statements were made in 1914, they are a faithful reflection of the prior Catholic stand, both before and after the Kulturkampf The different approach to traditional and modern Judaism finds clear expression in the remarks of Hans Rost, who wrote that "modern Judaism has freed itself from the strict conceptions and instructions which the Bible and the Talmud stipulated for marital law, both within and outside matrimony. The survival of Judaism for millennia is attributed to this strict observance. Fertility was perceived in the Old Testament as a blessing from God, and therefore God wished to multiply the seed of Abraham and Isaac. The great mentor of the Jews, the physician and rabbi Maimonides, laid down the laws on marital life and sexual relations according to the laws of nature and proper hygiene, and cited details in most discreet fashion. The Jew scrupulously observed these law for centuries. The laws are characterized by modesty, restraint and naturalness. The modern Jew has deviated from this way of life, and fallen victim to modern sexual permissiveness".[26] In contrast to traditional Judaism, the modern Jew was depicted as skeptical, materialistic and burdened by the curse wealth.[27]

The author regarded the Jewish question as dangerous, not because of its anti-Christian religious message, but because, due to its divisive social force, it constituted a threat to Christian society.[28] In such attacks the Jews were not discussed as individuals, but were judged collectively. As such, they were presented as a corrupt band of capitalists. It argued that capitalism had acknowledged the Jews to be protected modern legislation, as a national-religious collective unit, and in this fact was enfolded "their power and their social threat, since within the atomized general society (atomisierten Gesellschaft) they preserve their corporative nature."[29]

Catholicism perceived modern liberalism as its greatest foe, and in order to fight it, it took up the age-old cudgel of anti-semitism. All phenomena in society which were generally abominated were identified with Jewish traits, and liberalism was rejected through rejection of the Jew. The modern, reformist Jew, who sought to assimilate in Christian society and to abandon his tradition, was charged with responsibility for the 'secularization' of Catholic-Christian society. The modern liberal demand for separation of religion and state was also considered a Jewish idea. "Only in a state without religion (religionslosen Staat) does one find unbridled Jewish dominion."[30] "The reformist Jew is the personification of liberalism."[31] And the claim that it is not the Semites who are regarded as the enemy but liberalism is often reiterated. It is evident that in theory, this tactic was intended to exonerate the Catholic camp from charges of overt anti-semitism, but in practice, all the classic anti-semitic arguments were employed.

Catholic circles were severely critical of those Christians who had come under modernistic influences and had deviated from the path of the Catholic church. If they had not willingly absorbed the "poison of political liberalism" and as a result "themselves been transformed into Jews". They would not have reached the debased conditions in which "the Jewish spirit and the Jews in the flesh have become the masters of Christians."[32]

The attack on "reformist Israel" and on "the heretic young Israel" found clear expression in the sermons. The modern Jews, according to the preachers, had totally renounced the faith of their forefathers. Therefore, because of their insensitivity to religion, they had become an anti-Christian force. Those Christians who devoted efforts to achieving the emancipation of the Jews were, in the final analysis, tightening their own bonds.[33] The Jewish heretic was equated with the Christian heretic.

We see from this that in every circumstance, Catholic critique measured the standing of the Jew in Christian society by religious yardsticks. Sometimes this was done because the Jews were loyal to biblical tradition, and sometimes - because they rejected it. At times when Catholicism did not feel threatened by secularism, it rejected Judaism on theological grounds. When its status was undermined by secular modernism, it pointed to the modern Jew as the culprit. One way or another, the Jew and his tradition were perceived as a corrupting influence in society.[35]

NOTES

1.   Koerber, p. 287.

2.   Catholic Encyclopaedia, Vol. I, p. 634: "In the wake of Christianity's triumph under Constantine I the Great, anti-Judaism, hitherto theological and pastoral, took a political and legislative turn." See also Pfisterer, *ibid.*, Anti-Judaism.

3.   Fuhlrott, p. 94.

4.   Weiss, p. 526.

5.   Greive in Leo Baeck Schrifteneihe, Bd.33, p. 355.

6.   Knoll, p. 364.

7.   On the problem of the Emancipation, see Ruerup, and also Katz, Jewish Emancipation.

8.   Bachem III, 1927, p. 419; and see below *Die Wahrheit*, "Not hatred of Jews but defence of Jews."

9.   Lill in Rengstorf, p. 360.

10.   See under 'Juden' in Herder.

11.   See same item in the 1901-1905 edition of the same lexicon.

12.   According to research of Haase, p. 48.

       In 1907 480 Catholic political journals were published in the Reich, with more than two million subscribers.

13.   Tal, p. 56.

14.   Marr; the above quotations are from Zimmerman's article.

15.   Massing, p. 8.

16.   Marr, p. 7; Zimmerman, p. 138.

17.   Historische Politische-Blaetter, Vol 76, 1875, p. 221.

18.   Katolik, 52nd annual, 1872, Vol 35, p. 585.

19.   Historische Politische-Blaetter, Vol 85, 1880, p. 896.

20. *Ibid.*

21. Katholik, 53rd annual, 1873, Vol II, pp. 199-200.

22. Katz, Ghetto, p. 10.

23. See above p. 12.

24. Katholik, 22nd annual, 1812, Vol 86, p. 151, 152, 157. See also Philothea, 7th annual, 1843, p. 159. Stahl, p. 44.

25. Greive, Theologie, pp. 28-29.

26. Hans Rost, Der Zerfall des Deutschen Judentums, in Hochland, annual 2, 1913/4, 2, Vol 2, p. 547.

A Catholic periodical devoted to cultural affairs was published from 1903 on. It represented the trend to break through the wall of socio-cultural isolation surrounding the Catholic camp and to encourage integration in the modernization trends. From 1916 on it devoted most of its efforts to social issues.

27. *Ibid.*, p. 554: "The condition of our religious and moral German national culture would be much better were it not for the invasive influence of Judaism with its divisive and skeptical content, and the fervour of its criticism and materialism in almost all spheres of our life, both public and private."

28. *Ibid.*, p. 555.

29. Christlich-Soziale Blaetter 15th annual, 1882, p. 11n.

30. Christlich-Soziale Blaetter 12th annual, 1875, p. 398.

31. A Catholic, named Hugo Goerner defined the reformist Jew as "the personification of liberalism". See Organ fuer den Windthorstbund, November 15, 1898, p. 173.

32. *Ibid.*

33. Knoll, p. 364.

34. "The Jewish unbelievers, the "reformist Jews" have no interest in the messiah of the future, just as the heretic Christians have no interest in the messiah of the past." In Hammerstein, p. 201.

35. Philothea, 7th annual, 1843, p. 159.

CHAPTER TEN

THE JEWISH VIEW OF CATHOLICS

The Catholic attitude towards the Jews can also be ascertained from Jewish sources. Social contacts, whether established willingly or reluctantly, were inevitable, and they mirrored the outlooks prevailing among both the Catholic majority and the Jewish minority. The Jewish reaction indicates what role the Catholics played in their everyday lives, and is also a reflection of the Catholic outlook on Jews.

So far our discussion has been devoted mainly to the sermons delivered by priests and to the literature which they cited. Let us now examine the impact of these sermons on the everyday relations between the Jews and their Catholic neighbours. It is somewhat difficult to pinpoint the responses, since they were never specifically documented, and sometimes emerge only from asides and allusions in records and reminiscences.[1] Notwithstanding, it is possible to compose a picture on the basis of the memoirs of a Jewish community "which, in the main part, was composed of anonymous people, from the middle class, who had no great literary pretensions, but wished to leave a record for future readers."[2] These memoirs were written, not by Jewish scholars and intellectuals, but by "simple Jews" or, as they were denoted by their Christian neighbours, "village Jews" (Bauernjuden).[3]

In smaller towns and villages, contacts between Jews and Christians were necessarily closer and more intimate. The Christians perceived the Jews through the eyes and sermons of the local priest, as the following description indicates: "The peasant attributes all his tribulations, all his misfortunes to the Jew. Then comes the eagerly-awaited Sunday, and in church....he seeks to forget his troubles for an hour. Again he hears how the Jews crucified Jesus his saviour. The priest, who himself does not always know what to tell these simple peasants, describes the crucifixion in so terrible, so bloodthirsty a fashion, that it seems to have happened only yesterday. The peasant thinks 'That is exactly how they crucify me daily and rejection turns into hatred. It is not the fault of his meagre soil, his drunkenness, his large family, no, The Jew is to blame for everything."[4]

Necessity created close cooperation between all sectors of the small population, and the mutual dependence was evident in almost all spheres of life. These links, as various anecdotes show, were ambivalent: for the Christians, the Jew remained a being apart, because of his Judaism, while, for the Jews there was an invisible line which they did not cross. This line existed with regard to religion. The few Catholic priests who displayed good intentions with regard to their Jewish neighbours, they were rebuked by their superiors. It was made abundantly clear to them what their official stand should be towards the Jews and their religion. The following story, from a Christian source, is a typical example.

In the small town of Mutterstadt in the Speyer region, the Jews celebrated the inauguration of their new synagogue. The local priest, Dibelius, delivered a moving speech in honour of the occasion, which was reported by the local press.[5] He referred to the verse decorated the entrance to the synagogue "This is the gate of the Lord, the righteous will enter in." When this incident was made known to the supreme council of bishops then meeting in Speyer, Dibelius was ordered to explain his actions. The priest justified himself by saying that his sole intention had been to remind the Jews of their civil obligations, of which they should always be aware when entering the portals of the synagogue. The authorities however, were not satisfied with this explanation. Dibelius was summoned before a committee of enquiry, which put thirty one questions to him, which reflected the emphatic convictions of the interrogators on the matter:

"Should not the inauguration of the synagogue be regarded as a religious act?"

"Why did no Protestant clergyman attend the ceremony?"

"Did not the Catholic congregation in the town disapprove of the participation of a representative of the Catholic church?"

After the enquiry, Dibelius was informed that his attendance at a ritual Jewish ceremony was at odds with the policy of the church (unkirchlich) and was not acceptable (unziemlich).[6]

An Augsburg newspaper also took a stand on this affair. It declared that a member of the clergy was bound by his oath of allegiance to the church, to the teachings of Christ, whom the Jews had rejected and continued to reject. It was unthinkable, the paper wrote, for the priest to inaugurate a synagogue one day, and inform his flock on the next day that the sole salvation lay in belief in Jesus. Such conduct was a manifestation of hypocrisy.[7] Under pressure from all sides, Dibelius had no choice but to openly confess that his conduct had been basically misguided, and that in future he would not act in this fashion.[8]

In the absence of Jewish schools, young Jews attended Catholic schools, and were obliged to take part in lessons in Christian religion. The fact that catechistic literature was taught there, obliged the Jews to set themselves apart within the confines of their own religion. This counter reaction dramatically increased the religious and social tension between the two sides. Christian suspicions were directed mainly against the Talmud.[9] Erroneous and distorted opinions were proclaimed, reminiscent of those published by August Rohling, in his diatribe 'The Talmud Jews'.

The Prussian Royal Consistorium despatched a letter to the president of the Rhine district, demanding that a curriculum be drawn up which would be binding on Jewish pupils as well. The objective of the curriculum was to counter the anti-Christian incitement contained in the Talmud and introduced insidiously into the minds of Jewish children. The Jewish child, it was stated, was still educated in the spirit of the Talmud to regard the Christian not as a friend but as an alien; to believe that advantage could be taken of the mistakes of a non-Jew: to keep promises only if to do so was advantageous to Jews; to charge Christians usurious rates of interest. Since the Talmud disapproved of agricultural labour, manual labor was considered unfitting for a Jew. The declared aim was to change these objectionable views through a proper corrective curriculum.[10] (See Appendix D).

At the assembly of the Kingdom of Bavaria, two delegates, Clarus and von Gumppenberg attacked the leaders of the Jewish community and the Jewish educational institutions. "Do young Jews still hold the deluded view that the Jewish people alone are God's chosen people?" they asked.[11] The memoir which a Jew from the village of Bischberg wrote about his childhood reveals that Christian prayers and the tenets of the Christian faith were more familiar to Jewish pupils than Maimonides' thirteen tenets of faith When his teacher referred to "Christ's prophesy of the destruction of Jerusalem" and "Christ's signs from Heaven and the falling of stones from above", the intimidated boy asked his mother what this meant. She reassured him by saying: "We do not believe in these things, and what is not written in the Torah is not the truth..."[12]

Another Jew, who wrote his life story in 1867, told how, due to his impoverished situation after the death of his father, he decided to enter a Christian missionary institution. He bluntly described the sermons of the local priest as 'deception' (Augenverdrehereien). Constant study of chapter after chapter of Christian teachings, with their mystic content and absolute submission to the most extreme beliefs, drove him further and further away from Christianity, he wrote.[13]

The picture is one of co-existence fraught with tension. On the one hand, the needs of everyday life forced the two sides to cooperate. On the other hand, however, Catholic anti-Judaism cast its shadow on these relations. A Jew who found work as an apprentice in the glove industry, did not dare to reveal his origins. Only when his father died, and in order to honour his memory, did he reveal his identity to his employer and ask him to exempt him from work on the Sabbath. The employer agreed, according to the writer, only because he was 'a liberal Catholic'.[14]

There were interceders in towns and villages who tried to persuade Jews to convert to Christianity. A meeting was convened near Duesseldorf by the supreme body of an organization whose aim was 'to convert young Jews to the Christian religion'.[15] In another case, it was feared that the local priest might learn that a Jew had arrived in the town and "would not rest until he converted him."[16]

Priests were not always beloved by the Catholic population, sometimes because of their despotic conduct. The story is recorded of a local rabbi, loved for his pleasant demeanour; the Christians regretted that "the rabbi was not a priest".[17] This statement indicates something of the prestige enjoyed by priests within the community.

The modus vivendi between Christians and Jews can be seen to have been based on awareness of the existence of mutual interests. It was not that the Jew as such or the Catholic as such were admired and sought out; practical needs determined the nature of the social connection, Catholic employers in towns and villages sought skilled Jewish workers, and the Jew, for his part, needed work, and their interests often superseded the basic conflict between them, without obliterating it. The interests were not confined to the economic sphere, but related to education and social relations as well. In order to improve the standard of education in Christian schools, a certain priests was ready to amalgamate the "good school with the lesser one".[18] The rabbi of the small community rejected this proposal, arguing that the Christians were hostile to the Jews because of anti-semitic incitement, transmitted daily by the press, and this hostility would undoubtedly colour the attitude of Christian pupils towards Jews. The pragmatic approach of the priest was clearly manifested when he was asked by the rabbi to demonstrate his good faith by establishing social relations with the local Jewish physician. The priest replied: "How could I?...This man, as a Jew, is outside society, does not belong among ordinary citizens, and just if I cannot be on friendly terms with a policeman, thus how much more so with a Jew."[19]

Most Jewish testimonies emphasize the element of latent anti-semitism in society. On the one hand, they believed it to stem from the economic friction between the Christian day-labourers in villages and their Jewish employers. But on the other hand, it is evident that the breeding ground of this hostility was religious hatred, since "the everlasting belief in the Jewish culpability for the crucifixion of Christ has exacerbated anti-Jewish feeling."[20]

NOTES

1.   These sources are mostly taken from documentation collated by Monika Richarz in the introduction to her first volume, (hereafter Richarz A; B).   She writes of these documents: "Special emphasis was placed on the legacies of lower middle class writers, such as labourers, small traders, grade school teachers." (Richarz A, p. 17).

2.   *Ibid.*, p. 13.

3.   *Ibid.*, p. 173.

4.   Richarz, B, p. 163; see the interesting analysis by James Parkes, in his study of anti-semitism. Writing about anti-semitism in Austria, he notes the frustrations of simple people.   "The small traders who...proved more amenable; for the Jewish pedlar, the big Jewish shop and the Jewish capitalist industry could all easily be represented as the cause of their poverty and decline. The peasant also listened, for during the 80s and 90s the price of wheat fell, and this could be placed to the debit of the Jewish corn merchants instead of to its real - but remote- cause; the flooding of the world market with Canadian wheat." (Parkes, pp. 32/3).

A Catholic newspaper, in an article on the Jewish question in Alsace, writes as follows: "The peasant willingly attributed to the Jew all the catastrophes which befell him; for him, the Jew was connected to forces of nature: if a storm damaged his crop, if disease afflicted him, if the cattle perished - the Jew was to blame for all afflictions...in the eyes of the people, he was despicable, simply because he was a Jew from the same people which crucified Jesus and persecuted the Christians.   ("Die Wahrheit Vol 2, Munich, 1896, p. 411).

5.   Neue Speyer Zeitung, Beil. 230, 22 Nov 1838.

6.   Debus, pp. 264, 265.

7.   *Ibid.*, p. 268.

8.   *Ibid*, p. 266.

9.   See above, p. 48.

10.   See Debus, Vol 3, Letter dated March 14, 1824, p. 196.

11.   *Ibid.*, p. 246.

12.   Richarz, A, p. 168.

13. *Ibid.*, p. 180.

14. *Ibid.*, p. 188.

15. *Ibid.*, p. 180. An organization founded in Berlin in 1822. The meeting was convened at Elberfeld.

16. *Ibid.*, p. 190.

17. *Ibid.*, p. 362.

18. *Ibid.*, p. 157.

19. *Ibid.*, pp. 157-158.

20. *Ibid.*, p. 193.

CHAPTER ELEVEN

FROM THE 19TH TO THE 20TH CENTURY

The transformation of anti-Jewish prejudice in the twentieth century is clearly illustrated by the work of Julius Langbehn (1857- 1907), a German nationalist. He gained fame with the publication in 1890 of his book *Rembrandt als Erzieher - Von einem Deutschen*, which made a profound impression on the young generation of German Catholics.[1] In it Langbehn called for the revival of the German and Christian spirits.

The book contains a fierce attack on liberalism, intellectualism and the Jews. In 1900 Langbehn converted to Catholicism, and aligned himself with the more conservative forces, known for their fierce hostility towards the Jews. Prominent among them was the Bishop of Rothenberg, Paul Wilhelm Keppler, who denounced the Jewish influence on German society. In 1899, he declared: "The Jews are a thorn in the flesh of the Christian nations, and are sucking their blood."[2] The book was widely circulated, selling 100,000 copies in the first eight years.[3] It was considered highly topical since it reflected a dominant mood in German society: the heightening of irrational national sentiment, anti-modernist trends and the struggle against the rising tide of socialism. The combination of anti-western and anti-liberal ideas with Catholic beliefs, provided fertile ground for the spread of traditional anti-Jewish prejudice.

Many of the anti-Jewish images which we have found in nineteenth century sermons were already familiar in the Middle Ages. However, we are not concerned here with the historical aspects of Christian anti-Jewish theological theories but with the readiness with which the German public accepted the anti-Jewish propaganda of the Nazis and identified with their actions. Anti-Jewish theories, born out of the medieval Christian philosophy, found renewed expression in the modern Catholic (and Protestant) catechism and literature. Is it true to say that ecclesiastical anti-Jewish prejudice, as formulated in the nineteenth century, paved the way for Nazism? This is a valid question in light of the fact that at the peak of German imperialism, close to the outbreak of the First World War, organized anti-semitism was on the wane. German attention was then focused on the international arena, on the British, the French and the Africans. Only when the First World War shattered German imperialistic dreams did the Jewish question resurface in German society.[4] It should also be pointed out that, under the Weimar Republic, public anti-semitism was moderate in tone, and was not yet identified with extreme racist theories. On the other hand, Catholic prejudice endured. It was precisely the moderate character of the various parties in the Weimar Republic which made it possible to neutralize anti-semitism and separate it from the Nazi platform. Had the centrality of extreme anti-semitism in Nazi ideology been recognized at the time, Hitler might have lost numerous votes.[5] Documentation of the fluctuations of anti-semitic feeling is outside the scope of the present study, but there is one stable factor at all times. This is the durable anti-Jewish image, which was deeply imprinted on the minds of the general public. In 1925 the Jesuit Erich Przywara published an article, in which he charged the Jews with introducing secularism into the world, with worship of materialism and with suppressing pure religious faith. "Ahasueras, the worldly Jew" had taken the place of the celestial divine force.[6] During the Weimar Republic, racist nationalism was revived in Germany under various names such as "the ideology of the Volk" and "Volkism", which had been rife in Germany after the defeat of Napoleon Bonaparte. The term "Volk" or "Volkisch" was used by nationalists to refer to ties based on blood and race. This materialistic view was totally at odds with Christian theology, which regarded the Divine Will, rather than material elements such as blood and race, as the force determining human existence. However, there was another approach which found many supporters in Catholic circles, and that was the theory of the German "Reich". The origins of this concept lay in the philosophy of the mystic Joachim van Fiore (1132-1202), who predicted the advent of the Third and final Reich, where eternal peace would prevail. Catholicism translated this concept into "the descent of the religious entity into the midst of the temporal entity."[7] This earthly entity was understood by Catholic writers to be the "Third Reich", the unification of the Christian west (Christlichen Abendland) under the leadership of the German nation.[8]

The Catholic view of the "temporal" role of the Jews in this Reich, provided Christians with the opportunity to combine the racist-Volk view with their traditional anti-semitism. Matters reached such a pitch that a "Volk theory of Christianity"[9] was evolved. It sought to explain the singular biological traits of each and every nation as a manifestation of the divine scheme, expressed in blood and sex (Art und Blut).[10] According to this view, all nations were created "in the image of God" The Jews too were a part of this scheme, but had abandoned their divine mission. Their crime was considered twofold, both religious heresy and a denial of the racial world order. Thus, a racial element was introduced into the sphere of religion, and the spurning of the Jew on the basis of the theory of purity of blood was given religious sanction. It certainly cannot be said that most Catholics accepted the racial theory: only a small proportion were guided by scientific or theoretical racist considerations. The influence of the secular-- nationalist mood was clearly manifest in an article by a Catholic scholar from Dillingen in Bavaria. Discussing the Judaism of Jesus, he concluded that Jesus had not been a Jew. "Jesus was not born to a Jew but was the son of God." Racists later tried to argue that Jesus had been of Aryan origin, and it is interesting to note, in this context, the Catholic attempt to "free" Jesus of his Jewishness.[10a] The majority of Catholics still based their anti-Jewishness on aversion stemming from traditional standpoints.[11] But it was precisely this traditional loathing which was exploited by the racist nationalist associations which began to emerge in Germany at the end of the nineteenth century. An interesting example of these is the *Schutz und Trutz Bund*, which was active between 1919-1923, and helped pave the way for the rise of Nazism.[12] Its role in the dissemination of anti-semitism was considered an "all-German phenomenon."[13] Prominent members of this association sought ways to win over the clergy.[14] 'Volkisch' views had a particularly strong impact among Protestants. Official Catholic journals did not support the association overtly, but indirectly encouraged anti-Jewish incitement and called for pogroms against the Jews.[15] The Catholic Center Party and Bavarian People's Party tried to dissociate themselves from radical anti-semitism (see below). However, their Christian faith was permeated with prejudice, inculcated by preachers, particularly in rural areas.[16] Ludwig Hollaender, one of the leaders of the "Central Union of German Citizens of the Mosaic Faith" declared in 1919: "We have realized since the beginning of the revolution that we must endure terrible hatred of Jews and incitement to hatred of Jews, which are published in the press of the Central Party."[17] Among the Catholic mouthpieces which were particularly anti-semitic in tone were the church periodical, *Leo, Paderborn,* and the newspaper *Germania*. The tactic adopted from the outset by the founders of the "Schutz und Trutz Bund" persuaded many Catholics to join it. Since their aim was to recruit support throughout Germany, the founders omitted religious elements from their platform, and thus opened the door to Catholics. In the Paderburn area, it was reported that "Catholic priests, representatives of the church, intellectuals, and members of the higher echelons of the clergy have joined the association."[18] With time, as the racist element predominated over the religious viewpoint, some Catholics left the association in protest. The anti-Jewish element, however, was retained, and was the common denominator for the various components of the association. All the familiar anti-Jewish arguments voiced in nineteenth century sermons appeared in the association's platform. The familiar charges of "Jewish usury". the Judaization of the German banks and stock exchange, the 'Jewish-economic dictatorship in Germany', the Jewish financiers - were levelled against the Jews in order to prove their responsibility for the pre-war economic slump.[19] The onslaught on Jewish culture reflected dislike of modern trends in art: expressionism, surrealism etc, which were dismissed as manifestations of "the destructive Jewish spirit." The Jew was depicted as the corrupter of the theatrical arts, and Jewish mimicry was deplored. All these accusations are reminiscent of traditional anti-semitism. The question may be to what extent Catholics accepted or rejected pagan racist theories. It is manifest, on the basis of historical evidence, that the anti-Jewish indictments were identical in content. What had changed was the underlying argumentation. Modern research has shown that Catholic abhorrence of the Jews was deep- seated, - particularly in rural areas, among the untutored masses. It is not surprising, therefore, that the dividing line between traditional Catholic anti-semitism, and the hatred justified on racist-biological grounds (even though rejected by the Catholic leadership) was somewhat blurred. The despised Jew was ever present in the rural milieu. The reason why he was to be hated and reviled was immaterial. The sense of religious frustration was compounded by the element of mission which Hitler introduced into his anti-semitic diatribes. "I believe today that I am acting in the spirit of Divine Providence: by defending myself against the Jew, I am struggling for the Lord's Creation."[20] For the peasant, for the simple folk and even for educated nationalists, the racial principle became a divine edict where the Jews were concerned. Research on the attitude of German Catholics towards the Jews between 1850-1933, attributes great importance to the official stand of Catholic organizations in Germany. The leaders of the Catholic Center Party, Ludwig Windthorst and Ernst Lieber, generally tried to stem the tide of swelling anti-semitism. But, all in all, even if some Catholics defended Jews, this was done out of tactical considerations and party interests. As Lieber said: "As a minority in the Reich, we have not forgotten how we were treated, and for this reason...we will not lend a hand to the forging of weapons which will be used today against the Jews, tomorrow against the Poles and on the following day against the Catholics. Do not expect us to support you so that you can toy with the idea - 'we have rid ourselves of the Jews and now Bon voyage to the Catholics....'"[21]

In villages and small towns, the aversion to the Jews inculcated by the church remained profound. It should be recalled that the Catholics recruited most of their voters in those areas. It is not surprising, therefore, that the number of Catholics who were attracted to Nazism was particularly great in Bavaria.[22] The Catholic leadership took no steps to combat the anti-Jewish prejudices of this population,[23] and this inaction may have been due to reluctance to rouse controversy among these potential voters.

A scurrilously anti-Jewish leaflet, entitled *The Jewish Mirror* (*Judenspiegel*) was first published in 1883 in Paderborn, and disseminated in Westphalia and Bavaria. It was a purported collection of anti-Christian statements in the Talmud and Shulkhan Arukh. Within a few months, its circulation had reached 150,000. A third edition of a commentary on the *Judenspiegel* by J. Ecker, which ostensibly reaffirmed the anti-semitic findings, appeared during the Weimar Republic.

Towards the end of the Republic, forces other than the Volkist- racist ideology, operated to bring Catholicism and burgeoning Nazism closer together. Any discussion of this subject must take into consideration the dependence of the Catholic camp on Vatican policy. It was well-known that the Vatican was seeking ways to arrive at an understanding with Nazism, which it regarded as a militant partner in the battle against the true enemy, Bolshevism. The papal representative in Berlin, Monsignor Orsenigo, welcomed Hitler's rise to power.[24] The rapprochement was formalized in a concordat between the Vatican and the Nazis in 1937, and Vatican policy undoubtedly helped guide the footsteps of German Catholics. Also relevant is the fact that almost half the German population in 1939 were Catholics (43.1%) Even within the ranks of the S.S., almost a quarter (22.7%) remained loyal to Catholicism and did not leave the church.[25] The number of Catholics who were Nazi supporters was also significant. In 1932, more than two million Catholics voted for the Nazi Party.[26]

The Catholic stand during the Nazi regime has been studied and documented, and we can content ourselves with citing briefly some of the findings, in order to gauge the degree to which Nazi ideology was absorbed by Catholics between 1933-1939. Within the minor clergy, a priest named Karl Adam declared the theory of purity of blood to be an act of protection of Aryans, acceptable to "the Christian conscience."[27] The legend of the "stab in the back" was also revived in 1935 by Catholics. The journal of the Bavarian clergy, *Klerusblatt*, published an article under the heading "Marxism over Germany'. In it a Jew named Emil Barth was accused of treason for having supplied "his subhuman brethren (*Untermenschen*) with hand grenades and automatic weapons in order to attack the defenders from behind."[28] The Jews, it was declared "have a corrupting influence on religiosity and on the national character. They have a mortal hatred of Jesus and were the first and cruellest persecutors of the young church."[29] Hitler was considered "an emissary of God who has come to subdue Judaism."[30]

The anti-Jewish racial laws were regarded as essential, since they were aimed at preserving the quality of the German people.[31] Lewy concludes that "if we take into account this atmosphere of public opinion (among Catholics Z.B.) it is easier for us to understand why the church acquiesced in the face of Nazi anti-semitic legislation, even in areas where it encroached on church authority."[32] In the twentieth century, Christian public opinion in general absorbed the negative image of the Jew, which now became one of the cornerstones of the Nazi ideology waiting in the wings.

104

NOTES

1.   Stern, p. 227.

2.   Schemann, Vol I, p. 385.

3.   Stern, p. 200. In 1927, articles lauding Langbehn and his activities appeared in the journal Klerusblatt, the organ of the associations of Catholic priests in Bavaria, which allocated considerable space to current affairs and economic issues. These articles highlighted his role in fostering the German national spirit and praised his opposition to liberalism. Klerusblatt, No. 20, 11 March 1927, pp. 123-127; No. 27, March 12, 1927, pp. 140-142; no. 27, July 13, 1938, pp. 201-203; No. 3, 14 August 1938, pp. 225-227.

4.   Ernst I. Ehrlich, Judenfeindschaft in Deutschland, In Thoma, p. 235.

5.   Niewyk, p. 55, 61, 80.

6.   Niewyk, p. 56 and Greive, Theologie, p. 89, note 269.

7.   Sontheimer, p. 225.

8.   Sontheimer, p. 226.

9.   Greive, Theologie, p. 104, note 321.

10.   Greive, *ibid.*, note 318.

10a.   Klerusblatt No. 10, March 6 1935, p. 148.

11.   Greive, *ibid.*, p. 132, note 423.

12.   Lohalm.

13.   Lohalm, p. 120.

14.   Jochmann, Gesellschaftskrise, p. 149.

15.   Jochmann, *ibid.*, p. 151.

16.   Jochmann, *ibid.*, p. 159.

17.   Jochmann, *ibid.*, p. 407, note 315.

18.   Lohalm, p. 172.

19.   Lohalm, p. 140.

20.   Scholder, p. I 109.

21.   Pulzer, p. 274.

22.   Pulzer, p. 275.

23.   Rudolf Lill, Die Deutschen Katholiken und die Juden in der Zeit von 1850 bis z'ur Machtuebernahme's Hitlers, In Rengstorf, p. 386.

24.   Lewy, p. 27.

25.   Lewy, p. 292.

26.   Lewy, p. 18.

27.   Lewy, p. 279.

28.   Lewy, p. 396.

29.   *Ibid., ibid.*

30.   Lewy, p. 379.

31.   Lewy, p. 396.

32.   Lewy, p. 280.

CHAPTER TWELVE

THE CATHOLICS, HITLER AND THE JEWS

Numerous and diverse anti-Jewish elements can be identified in the statements and writings of the minor clergy and in homiletic literature. As we have seen, anti-Jewish theology was transformed into political ideology, whose aim was to serve non-ecclesiastical interests. The sum total of charges against the Jews and Judaism voiced in Germany reflected universal Catholic views and were not unique to Germany. But it was in Nazi Germany that the practical conclusions were drawn from centuries of consecutive vilification, conclusions which culminated in the planning and implementation of the mass murder of Jews. Thus, it is worth examining the impact of the Catholic outlook on Nazi anti-semitism. The question is whether historical and ideological continuity is discernible between Christian anti-semitism and the atrocities committed by the Nazis.

At first glance, the question appears irrelevant. There are great differences between the attitudes of Nazism and Christianity towards the Jews. In contrast to Nazi ideology, Christianity was interested in the survival of the Jews, in the hope that they would some day abandon their religion and convert to Christianity, thereby fulfilling Christianity's religious mission. It is a historical fact that very few Jews responded to Christian missionary efforts. The Jew's adherence to his tradition and refusal to accept Christianity brought down on his head the wrath of the Christian church, which perceived him as the ugly and corrupt Jew, setting himself against all that was good on earth. As long as Jews refused to acknowledge their error, the church

108

attacked them furiously, degrading and insulting them, but did not seek their death. This is the essence of Christian anti-semitism, and is not true of Nazism. The proclaimed aim of the Nazis was the physical annihilation of the Jews and the eradication of Judaism in general. There was an additional striking difference between the approach of the two ideologies towards racist theories. The church totally refuted these theories, thereby creating a rift with the Nazi regime.

German Catholics were unwilling to be included in the organized anti-semitic camp - either under the Second or the Third Reich. This was already true in Bismarck's day: Catholics joined the Center Party but avoided being officially denoted antisemites. They dissociated themselves from the anti-semitic sector since, as a liberal-anti-semitic group, it adopted a blanket stand against the Jews, the Junkers (the landowning and officer class) and the Jesuits. Any Catholic who joined their ranks would have been obliged to oppose his fellow-Christians, the Jesuits, thereby acting counter to his religious principles. Nor was there political justification for such a move. The Center Party did not openly declare its identification with anti-semitism, in accordance with the policy laid down by its leader, Windthorst. At the same time, many of its members were antagonistic towards the Jews, and their views were reflected in their newspaper, *Die Wahrheit*. An article entitled "Anti-semitism among German Catholics" stated, "We did not wish to be known by this name (antisemites Z.B.)...There is no contradiction here, since we do not dissociate ourselves from the objective identified with this name, but from what has been done in Germany in the name of this objective. This is what rouses our opposition....We have no sympathy for Jews...we can sum up our attitude towards the Jewish question by saying: not hatred of Jews but protection of Christians."[1] This diplomatic statement, which camouflaged anti-Jewish feeling under the guise of protection of Christians, and which fitted the dominant mood in German society, particularly at the end of the nineteenth century, -was relevant for many Catholics during the Third Reich as well. There was an additional reason why many Catholics preferred not to be known as antisemites. The explanation lies in contemporary events. One should distinguish between the period of the Kulturkampf, and the period from the end of the eighteen eighties onward. At the beginning of the Kulturkampf, Catholics denounced the "hostile attitude towards the Jews" (Judenfeindlich), seeking to dissociate themselves from the political and racial anti-semitism of the newly-emerged anti-semitic parties. They still considered the racial element to be indicative of "un-Christian anti-semitism."[1a] It would certainly be a misstatement of fact to claim that the entire Catholic camp supported Nazism. However, protection of Christians and promotion of the interests of the Catholic church undoubtedly took precedence over humanitarian concern for the fate of the Jews.

Influential German Catholics did not usually take the risk of protesting against the persecution of the Jews. A typical example is the attitude of Cardinal Faulhaber.* When requested by the Gestapo in Munich to clarify his attitude towards anti-Jewish racial policies, he replied evasively that he had indeed defended biblical Jewry in his sermons, but had expressed no views whatsoever on the modern Jewish question.[2] But even when the rumours of atrocities perpetrated against the Jews, were verified, the Catholic bishops did not take to the barricades. Cardinal Faulhaber realized that the church must raise its voice in protest. He approached his colleague, Cardinal Bertram* of Breslau and proposed that they compose a manifesto protesting the murder of Jews. Bertram's reply reflects the Catholic approach, namely that the church leadership should wield its influence, which he considered to be minimal, only on matters "of greater importance in the long term," particularly the burning issue of how to stem the destructive influence of anti-Christian and anti- ecclesiastical forces on the education of German Catholic youth.[3] This order of priorities demonstrates the place of the Jews in the German Catholic consciousness.

It would, as noted above, be difficult to prove the existence of a direct link between Catholic anti-Jewish actions and Nazi anti-semitism, nor can Catholics be held directly responsible for the Nazi atrocities perpetrated against the Jews. But the Catholics did play an important part in disseminating the negative image of the Jew, and in fostering unbridled hatred of Jews among Germans in particular, and in world public opinion in general. There was nothing new in Nazism's anti-semitic charges. Its racist ideology could just as well have been grounded on traditional anti-semitism.[4]

And not only was there nothing innovative in this propaganda. It should be clarified emphatically that there was an affinity between traditional anti-Jewish Christian theories and secular anti-semitism in general and Nazi anti-semitism in particular. This affinity reflects the ideological continuity between Nazism and anti-Jewish Christian doctrines. It is true that Christians were not partners in racist ideology or in mass murder. But where anti-semitism and anti-Jewish incitement are concerned, not only should the two ideologies be linked together, but - and this is even graver - one cannot understand the Nazi anti-Jewish viewpoint outside the Catholic-Christian context. There is a general tendency in certain circles to differentiate between the anti-clericalism which characterized racist-nationalist circles and Nazi ideology, and traditional Christian anti-semitism. The conclusion is that because of the contrast between them, they cannot be compared. It is more valid to say that "the Aryan-Semitic conflict is not a denial of the Christian-Jewish conflict but rather presumes its prior existence and absorbs it." Voelkisch circles in Germany were anti-ecclesiastical rather than anti-Christian. Anti-Jewish prejudices stemmed from the Christian heritage and remain imprinted on the public consciousness. The drift away from the ecclesiastical organization and establishment as a result of modern trends, does not necessarily imply departure from Christian elements.[4a] In this context, one cannot ignore the link between theological anti-semitism and Nazi anti-semitism, and Christianity cannot evade its responsibility for the existence of the interrelation between them.[5] In 1963, Cardinal Bea put his case bluntly: "The things which are being revived...are rendered particularly acute by the cruel slaughter of millions of Jews by the Nazi regime, and it is not within our authority to give exact figures. Special attention should be paid to this issue by the Second Vatican Council...This activity was accompanied by strong and highly effective propaganda; all this was made possible because this propaganda swept up believing Catholics, who were influenced by arguments originating in the New Testament and the annals of the church."[6] In 1964, at the Second Vatican Council, one of the participants, Bishop Elchinger of Strassburg, speaking of church sermons, admitted "that we cannot deny the fact that not only in our own century, but also in previous ones, crimes were committed against the Jews by sons of the church, and often falsely in the name of the church....and we also cannot deny that to the present day errors have often crept into sermons and catechistic literature, which are in contravention of the spirit of the New Testament."[6a]

Long before the rise of the Nazis, the harsh and hostile pronouncements of the church prepared German public opinion - from all strata of society - to absorb anti-Jewish slander and to identify with it. Hitler himself noted the connection between Catholic anti-semitism and his policies towards the Jews:

"I have been attacked for my treatment of the Jewish question. For 1500 years, the Catholic church regarded the Jews as pests (Schaedlinge) and despatched them to ghettoes etc. They then recognized what the Jews were. Under liberalism this danger was not yet acknowledged. I am returning to the deeds of that period 1500 years ago...Perhaps I am doing Christianity the greatest service."[7]

I do not know whether the church, for its part, considered Hitler's deeds to be "the greatest service". It may be assumed that it deplored the acts of genocide he committed against the Jews. But Hitler was operating on ground prepared for him by the church, and harvesting what Catholicism had sown. This is not to say that Hitler considered himself to be carrying out the church's policies.[7a] He abhorred its teachings, which he perceived as the total opposite of Nazi ideology. It was not the doctrines of the church but its organization which he admired, and he was ready to emulate its tactics in his war on the Jews. He himself attested to the fact that he adopted those ideas and methods which were useful for the implementation of his policies. "We absorbed our ideas from every twig and branch on the road of life, and we no longer know the origins of these ideas."[8] On his future plans, and to what extent he intended to learn from the church, he said:

"What can we ourselves do? Precisely what the church did when it forced its faith on the pagans: we will preserve what can be preserved, but will change the meaning. We will march backward: Easter is no longer the festival of the resurrection, but the eternal renewal of our nation. Christmas is the birth of our saviour and this is the spirit of courage and liberty of our own nation....The Catholic church is indeed a great institution. What organization! It has survived for two thousand years, and we must learn from

112

it....The church did not content itself with the image of Satan; it felt the need to translate it into a tangible enemy...the Jew... it is easier to fight him as flesh and blood that as an invisible demon."[9] Thus Nazism learned a lesson in tactics from the church but with the intention of altering the objective of the struggle.

Raul Hilberg, in his important work 'The Destruction of European Jews', sought to examine the bureaucratic apparatus which the Nazis employed in order to execute their murderous plans. At the beginning of his work, he conducted a comparison between the ecclesiastical bureaucracy which had operated for centuries, and the apparatus put into action by the Nazis. He justified this comparison with the following words: "If precedents have already been formed, if a guide has already been constructed, invention is no longer a necessity. The German bureaucracy could draw upon such precedents and follow such a guide, for the German bureaucrats could dip into a vast reservoir which church and state had filled in fifteen hundred years of destructive activity'.[10]

In the sphere of anti-semitic ideology, the Nazis were again able to draw on a reservoir of traditional hatred, which freed them from the need to invent hatred anew, and enabled them to follow in the footsteps of others while aspiring to different objectives. The Catholic- ideological precedent, like the bureaucratic precedent, constituted a basis for comparison which enables us to understand the readiness of the German public to absorb Nazi anti-semitism.

Let us now examine some of the similarities. Taking the Nazi attitude towards the ancient classical world, for example, one discovers that it was envisaged as a world of perfect beauty, of total perfection, whose aesthetic value far surpassed that of the spiritual worlds of both Judaism and Christianity. Hitler believed the pagan nations in the classical world to have been tolerant, because they did not worship one universal god, as did Judaism and Christianity. This demonstrates the inferiority of the Jew to the Greek and Roman.[11] Catholicism takes the opposite view. Paganism arrived at monotheistic belief through Judaism, but achieved perfection only when it accepted Christianity. The Jews were culturally above to the pagans, but in their turn yielded place to the Christians, who were superior to them. For

Hitler, the Jew was less than the pagan; for the Catholic - Judaism was inferior to Christianity. One way or another, the Jew is always inferior.[12]

The Nazi theory strove to prove that Jews were inherently corrupt, and, in doing so, employed methodology similar to that of the German Catholic catechism.[13] In the nineteen twenties, Nazi nationalist literature describes "the secret of Judaism" as the heritage of the Old Testament. Verses such as "For the soul of the flesh is in the blood, and therefore have I given it to you upon the altar to effect atonement for your souls, for the blood means: which oe's soul maketh one atonement." (Lev 17, 11) and the sacrifice of Isaac - were distorted by the Nazis. As far as they were concerned, these events demonstrated the murderous inborn traits of the Jew since, - thus they interpreted - non-Jewish sacrifices would be offered up in place of Isaac.[14] Hitler referred to the destructive character of the Jew. This description was common in nineteenth century sermons as well.[15] With Hitler, the theological accusation had now become racist and biological in character, and hence more absolute. In any event, the idea of the corrupt, destructive Jew, the murderous sinner - was by no means unfamiliar to the general public, of all walks of life.

Additional, more fundamental motifs which are present in the Catholic catechism, appear in new guise in Hitler's outlook. The idea of the 'chosen people' was central to both ideologies. Christianity - both Catholic and Protestant,- saw itself as the heir to the birthright of the Jewish people. It allotted the Jews the role of a superfluous, debased, and accursed people amidst the other nations of the world. Hitler adopted the idea of the invalidation of the Jewish people's status as chosen people, and his outlook, with its pagan manifestations, was based on it. "There cannot be two chosen peoples. We are God's people..." A Catholic preacher declared: "The birthright has been revoked.. and handed over to the Catholics for we are now the chosen people."[16] Hitler believed that there was polarity between "the people of the Devil" and "the people of God." Sermons and catechistic literature as well propounded the theme of the demonic Nature of the Jews. For Hitler, the Jew was the antithesis of all that was human, in contrast to the Aryan, while Christian teaching confronted Satan with Jesus. Those who reject Jesus are fighting the forces of good, and are identified with evil, just as the enemy of the Aryan is, as Hitler said, "outside nature and alien to it."[17]

The catechism charged the Jews, inter alia, with materialism. Our research has shown, on the basis of sermons and homiletic literature, that the catechism deduced Jewish materialism from the legalistic tradition. According to this argument, strict adherence to the letter of the law had stifled all aesthetic spirit in the Jew.[18] Over the centuries, there grew up the image of the "Mammon Jew", characterized by his covetous nature, worship of worldly things, and greedy exploitation of others. The literature on this theme is extensive and a few examples will suffice to illustrate it.[19] Hitler, as was his wont, absorbed the message and transformed it, in the spirit of Nazism, into an anti-Jewish diatribe. "The Jew Mordechai-Marx, being a good Jew, awaiting the coming of the Messiah". He placed the messianic idea within the framework of historical materialism, assuming that worldly riches are a component in the almost endless process of evolution. And elsewhere, "the deification of money", "Jewish profit" "Jewish materialism" are common expressions. In his monologues, he announced: "The Americans...when they receive gold in return for manual labour, store it in the cellar and assume that the world will follow this economic method, which originates in the Jewish spirit." "The Jew has no economic grasp, his thoughts are solely capitalistic." In general, Hitler often used the expression "moneyed Jewry" (Finanzjudentum).[20]

Jewish artistic creativity was also denounced. The Jewish ability to contribute to the arts was denied since, it was claimed, Jews had no aesthetic sense. These theories were grounded on the theological view of the Jews. Here again, a few examples can suffice to illustrate. Preachers declared that "the Jew has little interest in artistic and scientific aspirations." A Catholic journal cited Richard Wagner, who argued that it was impossible to conceive of a tragic hero or loving character being portrayed on stage by a Jew. If this were done, the audience would immediately sense the absurdity of the portrayal. The Catholic author admits that the Jews have nonetheless taken over the theatres, and are presenting Jewish operettas which violate the spirit of Christian morality. Jewish talent is best expressed in comedies, since this genre is suited to the Jewish temperament and character, whose power lies in imitation and pretence. After all, it was argued, in everyday life as well, the Jew employs these skills to deceive and cheat, since "all their aspirations are theatre. For the Jews life is a comedy, while for Christians it is a great tragedy." A local church periodical complains that the true sense of art (*echter-Kunstsinn*) and true interest in science have been lost, since all has been devoured by Jewish materialism.[21] From the church sermons, this anti-Jewish motif evolved until it was rediscovered in anti-ecclesiastical and non-ecclesiastical literature. In his well-known essay "On the Jewish question," the Protestant Bruno Bauer expresses the opinion that the Jew lacks the flexibility and the liberal spirit required for artistic and scientific creativity. Ernest Renan, the nineteenth century French linguist and orientalist, also expressed emphatic views on the artistic sense of the Jews. Writing of the "Semitic spirit," he claimed that the Semites lacked all creative imagination and were devoid of fictitious creativity. Their culture was identifiable by its negative characteristics: their works contain neither mythology, nor epics, nor science, nor fiction, nor philosophy, nor plastic arts. All these omissions stem, to his mind, from the Jewish-semitic monotheistic conception.[22]

There is no evidence in favour of the theory that Hitler drew inspiration from the Catholic catechism or the writings of Bauer and Renan: nonetheless, his remarks echo the Zeitgeist.[23] His views on the artistic talents and aesthetic spirit of the Jews could have been copied from theories prevalent before his time. In *Mein Kampf*, we read: "There was never a Jewish art, nor does it exist today. Judaism has made no original contribution whatsoever to the two queens of the arts - architecture and music. Its achievements in art...are spiritual theft. The Jews lack those qualities which mark the creative and the cultural elements in gifted races...The Jew is usually found in that art where the skill of self-invention is not evident - namely the art of the theatre. Here, he is revealed, at most, as a mimic...a pathetic comedian." In his monologues, he declared: "I have always said that the Jews are the most foolish devils who exist. They have not a single true musician. They have no art, they have nothing. They are liars, forgers and cheats."[24]

From Catholic sermons and literature and from Hitler's statements, one can draw up a list of the negative characteristics attributed to the Jews.

The list augurs the Holocaust to come. The central themes are focused on the nullifying of the status of the Jews as the chosen people, their satanic character, intolerance, inferiority, corruption, thirst for blood, destructive character, materialism, worship of Mammon, greed, lack of aesthetic and artistic sense, mimicry and cheating. We can but reiterate Hilberg's original statement in the context of the possibly affinity between Nazi and Catholic ideologies: "Necessity is said to be mother of invention, but if precedents have already been formed, if a guide has already been constructed, invention is no longer a necessity."[25]

Hitler drew the practical conclusions from the venomous denunciation of the Jews. There were no precedents for this genocide, and its occurrence may be regarded as the horrific innovation of Nazi anti-semitism. And if indeed no precedent for the Holocaust can be found in Christian anti-semitism, indirect sanction is implied in the sermons which nurtured public opinion. There it was said: "God did not wish this people - which deserved to be annihilated more than any other people - to be totally destroyed, in order that we should have living testimony of the truth of our holy religion."[26] A sociological survey by a Catholic author arrived at a rather extreme conclusion, namely that Bruno Bauer was right in stating that the existence of Judaism is an insult to the believing Christian. "Society can be cured of utilitarian religion only if the utilitarian people ceases to exist".[27] This is not to suggest that the author considered the physical annihilation of the Jewish people to be feasible. He was referring to the eradication of Judaism as a religion. This can be learned from the concluding remark "that the Jewish people must simply be brought to amalgamation (Amalgamierung)". It should be noted, however, that the author was not calling for the eradication of the utilitarian religion but of the utilitarian people. Hitler translated this sermon into action both literally and practically. The Christian considerations which motivated the Catholic sociologist were utterly rejected by Hitler. He believed that Christianity was outdated as were its dogmas. The "true religion" was now faith in Nazism, which had no further need of living testimony provided by the humiliation of the Jew. "This people deserves to be annihilated" but not because of Catholic-Christian considerations. Through their annihilation, Hitler sought to achieve his final aim: the establishment of a new world order.

The terminology used by Catholic preachers and writers was permeated with images taken from death, from the demonic world and from the insect kingdom, doomed to extermination. Hitler readily absorbed these ideas. He himself attested that "for one thousand five hundred years the Catholic church considered the Jews to be pests."[28] It is easy to imagine the force of the impact on the imagination and spirit of unlearned people and even educated believers, when they heard such descriptions as the following: "They (the Jews) were truly revealed to be cunning serpents, who, from their place of concealment, stung with their fatal venom; the descendants of their forefathers are a nest of vipers."[29] This identification of the Jew with demonic forces, with the Devil, is the expression of a latent wish, an unspoken desire to bring about the death of the Jew. Since, as the proverb says: "In the battle against Satan, - all means are justified."[30]

From the Middle Ages on, the church disseminated anti-Jewish propaganda, focusing on the motif of the demonic Jew, who is the Devil's partner, and his struggle against Jesus. A scholar who devoted a special study to the medieval Christian conception of the Jew and the Devil, wrote, inter alia, that the church inculcated in its flock the belief "that his followers must destroy the agents of the Devil...Christianity was summoned to a holy war of extermination, of which the Jews were only incidentally the objects. It was Satan whom Christian Europe sought to crush."[31] This tradition of demonization and dehumanization of the Jew, is ever-present in the sermons delivered by priests to their congregations. Hitler translated the following declaration (from a sermon) into the language of action, with the passive and active cooperation of numerous Christians: "This satanic generation was not destroyed when the Old Testament was forced to yield place to the New Testament; this hellsspawn (Ausgeburt der Hoelle) still lives... It sneaked from the Old Testament into the New, and spreads like poisonous weeds which cannot be eradicated, within the Christian community."[32]

Nazi propaganda films tried to present a visual image of the despised Jew. In the notorious *Jew Suess*, a parallel is drawn between the Jews, crowding together, and a flock of rats darting about among sacks of flour.

The associative intention is clear, and one might be excused for thinking that only the Nazi mind could have invented so perverted a comparison. But these images are to be found in nineteenth century Catholic writings as well. In one source, we find the statement that in order to understand the true meaning of a certain liberal article, one should translate each term into the opposite meaning. The following example is given: "In the language of the great stock exchange, a priest equals a rat. But the opposite of the priest is the Jew. Hence - Jew equals rat."[33]

One might ask what difference there is between the language of the churchmen and that of Hitler? Poisonous serpents, vipers, hells-spawn and rats are transformed in Hitler's lexicon into vampires, germs, blood-suckers, parasites.[34] It has been said regarding Hitler's assertions that "the language indicates the method" (*Und so legte schon die Sprache die Methoden nahe*). This remark is valid to the same extent for Catholic manifestations and the statements of anti- Christian German nationalists in the nineteenth century. The words of Paul de Lagarde may be regarded as the link between Christian hatred of Jews and Nazi anti-semitism. He attacks those who are too cowardly to "trample the spreading insects... one cannot negotiate with tapeworms and germs, nor can they be educated. They must be stamped out as soon as possible." The manifesto of the association of anti-semitic parties, published in Hamburg in 1899, contains a clear allusion to the extermination of the Jewish people; "Since the Jewish question, in the course of the twentieth century, will become a world problem, it must be solved finally (*endgueltig*) by the removal of the Jews....and in the end by the extermination of the Jewish people."[35]

Yet another parallel may be drawn. The Nazi leaders, including Hitler himself, tried to justify the murder of Jews on grounds of self-defense. The argument was that if the Germans did not rise up at once and eradicate the Jewish people, the Jews would turn on the Germans and destroy them. A Catholic periodical presented this idea in Christian guise: "Both the Book of the Zohar and the Shulkhan Arukh exhort the Jew explicitly to destroy Christians (*die Christen auszurotten*) and they perceive the advent of the Messiah as dependent on the extermination of the Christians." The fear of Jewish domination of Christians is also implicit in statements quoted above.[35a] The Jews, "like poisonous weeds, which cannot be eradicated" are depicted as a negative force, threatening Christianity. In present day Germany, a bitter debate is raging on revision of the understanding of the history of the Third Reich. Prominent among the revisionists is the well-known historian, Ernst Nolte. The 'defensive' element is central to his strange arguments. Nolte does not claim that the murder of the Jews was justified on grounds of self-defence against the Jewish threat, but, to his mind, it was permissible for Hitler to incarcerate the German Jews as prisoners of war, since, Chaim Weizmann had declared in 1939 that the Jews intended to fight on the allied side. Even stranger is his statement, which is ostensibly related to the theme of the present study: "Auschwitz is not essentially the outcome of *traditional anti-semitism* (Italics mine Z.B.) and was not in essence mere 'genocide'. What we have here is a reaction born out of fear at the destructive processes of the Russian revolution. This copy was far more irrational than the preceding original (since it would be a delusion to believe that 'the Jews' ever intended to destroy the German bourgeoisie or the German people) and it is hard to attribute to them so distorted an ethos. The copy was worse than the original because it perpetrated the destruction of human beings in almost industrial fashion...This explains the singular quality, but does not change the fact that what was known as the extermination of the Jews in the Third Reich "was but a reaction or distorted copy, and was neither a primary nor an original act." Nolte sees no continuity between traditional anti-semitism and the Nazi horrors, and explains the murder of the Jews as a response and a copy of the Russian atrocities. We are not concerned here with the debate as such. But it is important to indicate the trend to liberate hatred of Jews from its traditional roots and sources, and to explain it by considerations of self-defence which have nothing to do with the Jews themselves. Such revisionism, whatever its reasons, not only distorts the historical truth of the annals of the Holocaust, but also twists and distorts the history of the development of anti-semitism from ancient Christianity through the policies of the church and its dissemination of its catechism, to Hitler's death camps.[36] The connection between the Catholic attitude towards Judaism and the Jews and Nazi anti-Jewish policy is a tragic one. James Parkes has

120

pointed it out from a universal viewpoint, and his remarks enhance understanding of the German aspect of the problem:

"That which changed the normal pattern of Jewish-Gentile relations was the action of the Christian church. The statement is tragic but the evidence is inescapable. What is still more tragic is that there is no break in the line which leads from the beginning of the denigration of Judaism in the formative period of Christian history, from the exclusion of Jews from civic equality in the period of the Church's first triumph in the fourth century, through the horrors of the Middle Ages, to the death camps of Hitler in our own day."[37]

And indeed, under Hitler's tyranny, the cross collapsed, yielding place to the swastika.

NOTES

1. Wahrheit, Vol 2, 1896, p. 346, 347, 348.

1a. Tal, Christianity, pp. 58, 59, Jochmann, Gesellschaftskrise, p. 24.

2. Denzler, Vol I, p. 143.

3. Denzler, *ibid*,, p. 153.

4. Bacharach, Racism, p. 93.

4a. Greive, Theologie, p. 16; Tal, Christianity, p. 82, note 105.

5. Lewy, p. 269.

6. Freiburger Rundbrief, Ihrg. XV, January 1964, No. 57/60, p. 79.

6a. Lexikon fuer Theologie Vol II, p. 445.

7. Mueller, p. 129.

7a. Despite his basic objections to Catholic dogmas and his proclaimed abhorrence of Christianity, one cannot ignore the fact that Hitler was a Catholic, remained such and never left the church. Moreover: despite his persecution of churchmen, he was never excommunicated. Heer calls Hitler "an atheist Catholic" Heer, pp. 383/4.

8. Rauschning, p. 45.

9. Rauschning, pp. 58, 60, 234; Jochmann, Monologue, p. 321.

10. Hilberg, p. 4.

11. Jochmann, Monologue, pp. 96, 97; Bacharach, Massuah, pp. 25-31.

12. See above p. 30.

13. See above, p. 40 and the catechism on Jewish corruption.

14. Greive, Antisemitismus, p. 107; Jochmann, Monologue, p. 158.

15. See above p. 55.

16. See above p. 54; Rauschning, p. 238.

17. See above p. 60; Fuhlrott, Part 1, 1886, p. 238; Schmuelling, Vol I, 1882, p. 391; Deharbe/1, Vol II, 1861, pp. 359, 360.

18. See above p. 38.

19. Christlich-Soziale Blaetter, 1872, No. 1, p. 20; 1875, No. 12, pp. 8,397, 8,407; deliberations, p. 761; Knoll, pp. 185, 364.

20. Hitler, Mein Kampf, pp. 163, 212, 339, 702.

21. Wahrheit, Vol 5, 1899, p. 564; Christlich-Soziale Blaetter, 1850, p. 763; Hochland, Ihrg. 4, Vol 2, 1907, pp. 473, 476, Staatslexikon, 1927, p. 1657; Ehrler, p. 27.

22. "Le monothéisme et l'absence de mythologie expliquent cet autre caractère fondamental des litteratures sémitiques, qu'elles n'ont pas d'épopée...la race semitique...elle n'a ni mythologie, ni épopée, ni science, ni fiction, ni philosophie, ni arts plastiques, ni vie civile...L'intolérance des peuples sémitiques est Ia consequence necessairs de leur monothéisme." Renan, pp. 11, 12, 18.

23. Bracher, p. 66, "Hitler never gives concrete information on the literature he read".

24. Mein Kampf, p. 332; Jochmann, Monologue, p. 131.

25. Hilberg, p. 4.

26. Deharbe/1, Vol 4, 1869, p. 150.

27. Boenigk, p. 154.

28. Mueller, p. 129.

29. Patiss, p. 696.

30. Heer, p. 338.

31. Trachtenberg, p. 21/2.

32. Philothea, Jhrg. 15, No. 50, 1851, p. 394.

33. Die Sittenlehre des Talmud, p. 178.

34. Mein Kampf, pp. 331, 334; On use of the term 'parasite' in anti-semitic literature, see Bein.

35. Jaeckel, p. 75; Lagarde, p. 209; on these remarks by Lagarde, see Stern, p. 93, note: "Nor did the National Socialists forget this prophecy. In 1944, when they were carrying out their policy of extermination, an anthology

of Lagarde's work was distributed by the army, and contained Lagarde's demand for murder."

35a.   See above, note 32, Wehler, p. 112.

36.   Mein Kampf, p. 702; Hoess, Commandant of Auschwitz, wrote in his diary that Himmler summoned him to Berlin in Summer, 1941, and entrusted to him command of the death camp. In his explanation, Himmler said: "All Jews, without exception, who are now in our grasp, must be exterminated in this war. If we do not now succeed in destroying the biological foundations of Judaism, the Jews will some day arise and destroy the German people." Hoess, p. 157; Historikerstreit, p. 32/3, 24.

37.   James Parkes, Anti-semitism, p. 60.

CHAPTER THIRTEEN
CHRISTIAN RESPONSIBILITY

Our focus on the attitude of the Catholic population towards the Jews of Germany does not preclude examination of the stand of the Catholic church in general towards the Jewish question. As noted above, attitudes towards the Jews were similar in different countries. It was the events of the Holocaust, as a unique chapter in the history of Germany, which led us to concentrate on the German people. While the minor clergy and local churches often acted relatively independently, and even in contravention of the official line, (e.g. concerning blood libels or theories on the advent of the Antichrist), one must nevertheless take into account the overall outlook, policies and doctrines of the Catholic church, as formulated over the centuries by the architects of Christian theology. In the final analysis, it was this outlook which created the image of the Jew as envisaged by the general public. In contrast to the encounter between the ancient world and the Jews, the Christian message is characterized by its universal aspect. Greek and Roman particularism was manifested in the rights and obligations of the citizen vis a vis his state. Christianity, in contrast, preached the submission of man, the citizen of the world, to the Lord of the Universe, whose dwelling place was above and beyond this earthly sphere.

The distinction between particularism, between ancient man's awareness of his own historical centrality, and the sense of universal mission which characterized the new Christian believer, has been pointed out by Collingwood.[1] This universal history does not perceive events on earth, historical happenings, as the outcome of the intentions and wishes of man, but as the expression of the Divine will, over which man has no control. As Collingwood has said: "It is a play written by God". This is an apocalyptic history revolving around the character and actions of Jesus. It focuses on the description of his past and on the eschatological vision at which his deeds are directed. According to the Christian approach, the revelation is the regulator of human history - from the Creation in the past to the future kingdom of the Messiah. Flusser explains that "Jesus as Messiah is important today mainly to those who await his imminent advent, while the claim that Jesus was the Messiah is voiced mainly by Christians in their appeals to Jews to acknowledge Jesus as their Messiah - that is to say in the past."[2]

The significance of this eschatological outlook for the history of the Jews is of decisive weight for our subject. The question which arises is what place to allot to the Jew within the framework of this outlook. Christianity stems from Judaism, and, as Flusser says, Jesus was a Jew, lived in the Jewish faith and died for its sake.[3] Again, we should not forget that the Bible, the Book of Books of the Jews, the 'Old Testament', was sacred to Christians. In light of these facts, one might have expected ancient and of later Christianity to respect and esteem the mother-religion in particular and Judaism in general. But history has shown - and we may take this as a fact - that "the attitude of Christianity towards its heritage is ambivalent. On the one hand, there is the desire to be the 'true' Israel, on the other there is no desire to identify with Judaism and particularly not with the Jews."[4] However, it must be admitted that, in the end, the desire to be the 'true' Israel was transformed into aversion to Judaism. Why did this attitude turn sour and negative, expressed in denunciation and vilification, culminating in savage and bottomless enmity from which the world has yet to extricate itself? Some enlightened Christians have been driven by conscience into making such statements as the following: "More than six million deliberate acts of murder are the result of teachings about the Jews, for which the Christian church is responsible in the final analysis, the outcome of an attitude towards Judaism which has not only been advocated by all Christian churches, but whose roots lie in study of the New Testament itself."[5] The apocalyptic approach asserts that everything that occurs in this world, the actions of each and every individual- are but episodes which together make up a totality, which aspires towards a better world as promised by the Christian saviour. The way in which this view is reflected on the historical-earthly plane, has been illustrated by a historical parable: according to this parable, it may be assumed that it was possible to assassinate Julius Caesar, but impossible to prevent the fall of the ancient Roman republic by this act.[6] The sole significance of the assassination lay in the bestowal of historical characterization on that fall.

In the process of historical occurrence, the protagonists are judged according to apocalyptic standards. Collingwood rightly cites, in this context, the famous saying of the poet Freidrich von Schiller: "Die Weltgeschichte ist das Weltgericht" (The history of the world is but the Judge of the world).[7]

The protagonist in this fixed historical pattern is a passive figure, activated from outside by an extra-human, superhuman force. This is the transcendental Christian view of the history of mankind. Divine power does not act immanently, within and through human agents, but rather extraneously. Human temporal experience is translated to that sphere which is above and beyond the human. Those who do not accept the Christian creed, who resist this trend, are rebelling against the Divine scheme, while at the same time unable to change it. For the Christian, the Jew is the supreme rebel, since he is rebelling against the messianism of Christ. He undermines the heavenly plan since he is steeped in worldliness, in human immanence, and rejects transcendence. But, worse still, since he is unable to change and divert divine intention, his faith, rebellion and heresy are purposeless, barren - in short, a great sin against divinity.

Herein lies the core of the negation of Judaism and of the heretic Jew, who dares to challenge the divine good. To accept Christian theology is, of necessity, to reject the Jew because of his Judaism. According to the Catholic conception, man is born in sin. His salvation depends on the miraculous revelation of God's grace: baptism, the mass and the other sacraments, and all the miracles, all these can raise the believer above his earthly defilement. Jewish teachings are the complete reverse of these Christian theories. According to Judaism, God does not bestow his grace on mortals, but demands constant action on their part. This demand is based on the awareness that man is not a sinner from birth and is able and willing to choose to do good. His salvation, and, it should be noted, the Jewish messianic approach in general, are functional vis a vis human morality and free choice.

The implication of this conflict of views is that Christians regard the Jews as sinners who have been tried by God, and condemned to the obliteration of their Judaism and, in the end, of their personal dignity.

In light of this Christian outlook, one might ask why so much attention should be focused on the invalid deeds and actions of the Jew? This question is relevant not only for the fate of the Jew, but also, by force of the apocalyptic outlook, for the role and actions of any human being within the universe. However, Christian theology distinguishes between the Jews and all other human beings. The distinction stems from the fundamentally conflicting approaches of the two religions.. Catholicism believes in the Original Sin and in man's passive role in this world. His existence is humble and submissive in a sinful world, and he lives in constant expectation of a better messianic future, at some unknown time. He must place his trust in the divine miracle, and therein is epitomized his life on earth. The Jewish religion refuses to acknowledge the insignificance of man, since he was created by God, and the apocalyptic element is marginal in his faith. The Jewish path is elucidated by the following statement: "We learn from the Book of Exodus, Ch. 13-17 one very great thing, and that is that the miracle, the revelation and the raising of man to poetic heights in light of the miracle of revelation - is but a fleeting episode, which has no impact on what is to follow, and what endures is not the poesy but the prose of life.... and the miracle and all supernatural factors are revealed to be religiously meaningless, and, in any case, are not effective vis a vis the consolidation of faith. The generation which witnessed the miracles and the wonders - did not believe...that we know there were many generations, dozens of generations of Jews in which many, and not only a chosen few, worshipped God and his teachings and were willing to sacrifice their lives for Him. These were generation to whom the Divine Presence was never revealed, and who never witnessed miracles....and yet they believed. Faith is not bestowed on us from without, nor can it be thus bestowed. It can grow only through the efforts of the individual, his resolve and his decisions..."[8] Temporality, the realities of this world, are central to the religious convictions of the Jewish believer. His actions in this world are the true manifestation of Divine worship. This is the 'true' Israel according to the Jewish outlook, while Christian theology hopes that the Jew's voluntary acknowledgement of his degraded condition on earth will pave the true path to Christianity for him. Refusal to accept Christianity will of necessity lead to abasement of the Jews, until they agree to accept it. But, as we know, Judaism did not acknowledge the truth of Christianity. The desire of Christians to become the 'true' Israel eventually led to the crusade against the 'false' Israel.

In exposing this aspiration, we reach the heart of the relations between Christianity and Judaism. Why did theological objection evolve into such virulent hatred, and how did it become the basis of universal anti-semitism? One original explanation seeks the answer in the fact that the annals of Christianity are based on failures. One of these was the crucifixion of the saviour, whose disciples fled for their lives. This phenomenon, of a religious movement which converts its failure into strength, has parallels in history. Shabtai Zvi, who failed in his mission and converted to Islam became, for his disciples, the symbol of a messianic movement of great power and influence. Hence, failure in the religious sphere can generate great power, since the believer is now maintaining something which never reached fulfillment in its original form. He is required to mobilize superhuman inner forces to continue to believe in something which he knows, deep in his heart, to be unfulfilled.[9]

This transformation of defeat into victory had far-reaching consequences for the development of socio-cultural ties between the Gentile and Jewish world throughout history. Christian fury was now directed against those who were responsible for the failure. An example of the vicious attacks on the Jews by the Church Fathers is the statement by Chrysostom in the fourth century CE, of which it was said: "It is evident that Chrystostom's Jew was a theological necessity rather than a living person."[10]

The church had need of the image of the Jew as an ideological component in its religious doctrine. This fact is important for comprehension of the status of the Jew within Christian society. There is now no need for the physical presence of the Jew; what matters is the image of the Jew as perceived by the Christian believer. This distorted image of the corrupt Jew served the needs of Christian theology, but also presented a great difficulty. "Israel by flesh" is the historical earthly Israel which adamantly refused to acknowledge the truth of the Christian religion. His continued existence despite his refusal to acknowledge the messianism of Christ, threatens the superiority of the Christian religion. This was the reason for the advocacy of the "theory of degradation", according to which the Jew must be humiliated and despised by all nations. This same degradation is the living proof, the "theological need", bearing witness to the triumph of Christianity. Reflected in the everyday life of the Jew, it prepared the ground for future persecution of and discrimination against the Jew.

The second failure of Christianity was the fact that most Jews were unwilling to join its ranks. Their adamant rejection made an enemy of the proselytizing Christian and led to demonization of the Jew. By resisting absolute Jesuit good, the Jew became the personification of absolute evil. There are no compromises where divinity is concerned, and the choice is unconditional. This absolutist view of the traits and character of the Jew is of central significance for the history of Jewish-Christian relations. It helps explain the force and might attributed to Judaism and to Jews. Underlying this view of the Jew as a creature of diabolical capacity, the partner of the Devil, is belief in the great power- albeit negative -of the Jew. The antithesis of the forces of good is the evil Jew who seeks domination. Examination of the fabric of these relations since the birth of Christianity, reveals different versions of this view. We find the Jewish usurer, the Mammon Jew, the international Jew, the power-hungry Jew of 'The Protocols of the Elders of Zion', the Jew who is influential in culture, or - according to the biological image of Nazi anti-semitism - the Jew as parasite. I permit myself to speculate further, and state that the modern image of the "cruel" Jew in Israeli army uniform is one of these false stereotypes, which have one common denominator: the desire to draw a picture of a powerful threatening force. Therein lies the justification for humiliation and persecution and, in the end, for murder. Herein, too, lies the key to understanding of the creation of prejudice against the Jew. The Christian, who is obliged to convince himself of the validity of a phenomenon which failed him, is forced to reinvent the longed-for reality, even if this invention refutes all logic. He will judge his surroundings on the basis of his assumptions rather than of real facts. This is the essence of all prejudice: to deduce a value judgment on the basis of inferences and wishes rather than facts. Apart from its spuriousness, prejudice holds out an additional danger. Its efficacy depends on its acceptance by the majority.[11] It can exert its negative effect if it is universally accepted, whether the majority is composed of Christian believers or anti-Christian Jew-baiters.

In the process of absorption, the borderline between hypothesis and fact becomes obscure, or, to be more precise,- in the public consciousness, hypothesis is equated with fact. One could trace the course of history and examine the many instances in which the hypothesis was presented as fact. One could cite many examples of this process in the course of history how the acceptance of the temporal world by Jewish religious philosophy was interpreted as materialism and worship of Mammon; how rejection of the Christian messianic ideal was transformed into the act of crucifixion and later, into the facts' of the blood libels etc.

The total negation of the deeds and religious beliefs of the Jews created the amazing phenomenon whereby the Jew became both the antitype and the antithesis. For the capitalist, he is the socialist or communist, but for the latter he personifies capitalism. He is an outcast everywhere, dispersed and exiled, and at the same time is accused of ruling the world. One could cite endless examples of this.[11a]

With time, the Catholic church forfeited some of its power, and secular forces began to emerge in Europe from the 17th century onward. With the dwindling of Christian power and influence, hatred of Jews might have been expected to wane as well. There were indeed periods in which religious hatred lessened. But the negative image was so deeply rooted in the popular consciousness, that it endured "in its own right" It was adopted by modern historical figures, some of whom were opponents of Christianity. The socialists Charles Fourier and Pierre Proudhon; Ernest Renan, Karl Marx - all these exploited the negative image of the Jew to reinforce their ideologies.

132

The greatest enemy of the Jews in the history of mankind, Adolf Hitler, knew where to turn when he sought to explain and justify his anti-semitism. We have already quoted the statement in which he took pride in serving the interests of the church in his war against the Jews.[12]

The process of transition from traditional Christian anti-Jewishness to Nazism is heightened when one is aware of the similarity between them. Both needed an enemy, an antitype. They were required, in order to survive and justify their existence, to translate the image of the Jewish enemy as created by prejudice, into the everyday, mundane Jewish enemy antagonist. Hitler openly asserted that he learned this tactic from the Catholic church. The central components of the Christian view of the Jew and Judaism served as the basis for consolidation of the anti-Jewish ideology of the Nazis and were transmuted by its policy makers. The Jew as foe of the Christian God was perceived by the Nazis as the enemy of the Aryan type.

The negation of Judaism was essential for justification of Christian superiority. Hitler sought to bring about the salvation of the German-Nordic race through destroying Judaism. Nazi ideology was able to base its attacks on the Jews on prejudices shaped by Christian theology. The Jew, as powerful, omniscient enemy was regarded by both ideologies as a threat to the world order.

The sufferings of the Jews in world history are anchored in these facts. Even if Christianity did not call for the death of the Jews, since it had "theological need" of them - one cannot ignore the fact that this was an a posteriori need. The degradation of the Jews was the substitute for their extermination. Christianity could not demand the killing of the Jews - even though this act was the logical outcome of the principles we have noted, since their extermination would have cast doubt on the Christian demand to be considered the legal heir of the Jewish creed. "No jury would agree to grant a legacy to someone who won it through murdering the testator."[13] If we continue this train of thought, we discover that the difference between Hitler and Christianity is that the latter chose the path of degradation of the Jew out of its own particular interests, while Hitler humiliated and murdered as well. The tragedy is that substantiation for both policies can be found in Christian theology.

Some Christians have tried to rectify the misconceptions about the Jews, particularly since the Holocaust. But if one examines some of the more important pronouncements of the Vatican, it appears that, rather than revoking previous stands - they reinforce them.

The 1964 Vatican Council passed resolutions aimed at launching a dialogue between Jews and Christians, in the wake of Pope John 23rd's courageous attempt of 1963. But the text of the amendment in the Nostra Aetate document requires careful perusal.

"True, the Jewish authorities and those who followed their lead pressed for the death of Christ; still, what happened in his passion cannot be charged without distinction against all the Jews then alive, nor against the Jews of today. Although the Church is the new people of God, the Jews should not be represented as rejected or accursed as if this follows from the Holy Scriptures."[14]

True, not all the Jews are guilty of the crucifixion. This is a new attempt to make amends for an ancient tradition. But what can one say about the statement that "the Church is the new people of God?" Is this not a return to the desire to become the 'true' Israel, and a reaffirmation of the basis for all the prejudices against the Jews?

Guidelines and explanations for the Nostra Aetate were published in 1975; there too one finds dogmatic principles, anchored in Christian tradition, though disguised by moderate terminology. The church must disseminate Christ's message, but this dissemination should not involve aggression against the Jews. It is vital to take into account the problems encountered by the Jewish spirit when presented with the secret of the Incarnation or what the document calls "the word made flesh". It is stated that Judaism perceives Divine Providence in spiritual fashion.[15]

The implication is that the true religion is that which acknowledges the Incarnation of Christ. On the difference between the ancient stance of the church and the views formulated after the Holocaust, it is said: "The objective of Judaism's existence and its right to exist lie, therefore, according to the ancient edict, in its eradication. The new element in the church's outlook is therefore that it expects the Jews to admit the validity of this

134

ancient edict; but now not from a condition of inferiority but from a standing of equal rights, as part of the modern world".[16]

And thus the question which Jean Paul Sartre[17] asked Christians, remains relevant: "What have you done to the Jews?"

NOTES

1.   Collingwood, p. 49: "Any history written on Christian principles will be, of necessity, providential, apocalyptic and periodized. It will be universal history, or history of the world, going back to the origin of man. It will describe how the various races of men came into existence and peopled the various habitable parts of the earth. It will describe the rise and fall of civilizations and powers. Greco-Roman Oecumenical history is not universal in this sense, because it has a particularistic centre of gravity. Greece or Rome is the centre round which it revolves. Christian universal history has undergone a Copernican revolution, whereby the very idea of such a centre of gravity is destroyed."

2.   Flusser, Christianity, p. 19.

3.   *Ibid.*, p. 448.

4.   *Ibid.*, p. 449.

5.   Hay, p. 15.

6.   Collingwood, p. 53.

7.   *Ibid., ibid.*

8.   Leibovitz, Notes, pp. 48/9.

9.   Flusser, Mahanayim, p. 26.

10.   Parkes, Conflict, p. 166.

11.   Parkes, Anti-semitism, pp. 161/2.

11a.   See above, p. 51.

12.   Mueller, p. 129; see above p. 90.

13.   Flusser, Christianity, p. 449.

14.   The English text is from Encyclopedia Judaica, Vol, 5, p. 550. Rabbi Abraham Joshua Heschel, leader of American Conservative Jewry, published a response to the Vatican proclamation in *Time*, 11.9.1964. He said, inter alia: "As I have pointed out time and again to senior Vatican dignitaries, I am ready at any time to go to Auschwitz if faced with the choice: conversion or death...."

15.   This is the text of Document No. 3, January 3, 1975, which contains Vatican instructions for the implementation of the resolutions of the Second Council, Nostra Aetate.   Translation in 'Freiburger Rundbrief, Ihrg. Yearbook XXVI, No. 97/100.

16.   Tal, Patterns, p. 28.

17.   Sartre, Reflexions, p. 83.

CONCLUSION

I have not attempted to give a systematic and chronological picture of the relations between Jews and Catholics in nineteenth century Germany. The aim has been to highlight the basic elements in the outlook of Catholic priests and mentors, as reflected in statements and sermons. It was difficult to track down sermons, and there is no way of knowing why some were published and others not. Some preachers may have won a name for themselves due to the popularity of their sermons, and consequently their texts were published on the recommendation of their local archbishops. Such recommendations constituted official sanction for the sermons. Analysis of the geographical dispersion of the villages and towns where the preachers delivered their sermons, illustrates the wide dispersal of their views on the Jews.[1] An important source of information were the various manuals of instruction consulted by preachers and householders in general. Since we are dealing with official literature approved for use by clergy and by educated Catholics, it can serve as an indicator of ideas, trends and views prevailing within the population.

Generally speaking, these statements reflected the theological principles established by the Church Fathers. These principles have been exhaustively documented and studied by such well-known scholars as Joshua Trachtenberg, James Parkes, David Flusser and others. It was not our intention to delve into theological issues as such or to discuss the fundamental conflict between Christianity and Judaism. Our question was: how did Catholic theology influence the course of the history of anti-semitism in Germany. We were concerned with the possible impact of these Catholic views on the shaping of German public opinion, and its attitude towards the Jews in Germany. Such examination contributes to understanding of the absorption of anti-Jewish views by wide sections of the population in the second half of the nineteenth century, preparing the ground for Nazism in the twentieth century. The anti-Jewish pronouncements in Catholic churches, and the inflammatory statements in catechistic literature, were dogmatic and emphatic, and were presented to churchgoers as divine edicts. And since they were accepted as absolute statements stemming from the divine will, they were perceived by the public at large as unquestionable truths. When the Nazis came to power, they allocated hatred of Jews a central role in their ideology. Nazi anti-semitism activated Christian hostility and addressed Catholics (and Protestants) in familiar and common language. This leads us to the conclusion that the Nazi crimes against the Jews should be viewed as one piece with Christian anti-Jewish elements as regards background and cause. One should not infer from this that the Catholic church and all its organizations were direct partners in the extermination of the Jews. But the Nazi murderers were nurtured on Christian anti-semitism, and it came as no surprise to the general public in Germany when they translated previously known theory into practice. The special circumstances of the German historical tradition absorbed Christian anti-semitism, and in this fusion is epitomized the unique path of German history.

On the other hand, this does not imply mitigation of the guilt of the Nazis. The direct responsibility for the implementation of mass murder of the Jews rests on their conscience and that of those who supported and aided them. Catholicism, - and certainly also Protestantism, which has not been discussed here - played an indirect part in this guilt, paving the way and preparing the ground. The immensity of the horror of the Nazi atrocities has overshadowed awareness of the dangers of the prejudices which preceded them, which, relatively speaking, were the lesser evil.

We have attempted to show how great was the force of the Catholic-Christian prejudice. It set the Jew apart from the rest of mankind and poisoned the hearts of millions of Germans. This doctrinarian brainwashing facilitated Hitler's scheme for winning support, since his language was familiar.

NOTES

1.   The sermons quoted here were delivered in the following small towns and villages: Klein-Suessen, Neuss, Dornbirn, Ingenbohl, Lautingen, Kirchwobis,   Kirchheim,   Roedelheim,   Machrisch-Truban,   Fiecht, Reichenberg, Reisbach, Zuelpich, Moenchengladbach, Osnabrueck, Buehl, Uffikon, Lindau, Tirschenreuth, Paar, Huefingen, Trier, Mockensdorf, Schwoerzkirch, Rothenburg, Apfeltrang, Steindorf, Eppelborn, Tiefenbach, Deggendorf, Seligenstadt, Starnberg, Limburg a/L.

The preachers were influenced by trends in the urban Catholic centers, such as Koeln, Paderborn, Freiburg, Muenster, Muenchen, Mainz, Wuerzburg, Tuebingen, Augsburg.

APPENDIX A

From Kroenes, Vol. 9, 1860, p. 345ff

Moses

Jesus

Appeared amidst his brethren with signs and miracles as emissary of God (Exodus 4, 1-9)

Thus also Jesus; and hence he appealed to the Jews to believe in his deeds (John 10,38)

Freed the Jews from the temporal slavery of Pharaoh (Ex 11, 24-29)

Freed us from eternal servitude to Satan

Chose the elders of Israel from among the people (Ex 17, 5,9)

Chose 12 apostles and 72 disciples to spread his teachings and rule God's church (John 1, 37-49)

Brought the Ten commandments from Sinai after spending 40 days and nights in a cloud (40,31,18)

Spent 40 days and nights in the wilderness and brought us the laws of the New Testament (Matthew 4, 1-11)

Jonah

Jesus

Guilty, was cast into the sea and spent 3 days and nights in the belly of the whale from which he emerged alive (Jonah 2, 1, 11)

Though innocent, went to his death with the sins of mankind weighing on him. Spent three days in the tomb and arose on the third day (Matthew 12, 29, 40)

David

Jesus

After trails and tribulations, when his son rebelled against him, returned as conqueror to Jerusalem, and was lauded by his subjects (Kings 2, Chapter 22)

Jesus too returned to Heaven in triumph after suffering and humiliation on earth having died a despicable death through betrayal by a disciple, and there he was lauded by all the angles (John 3, 16)

142

Noahs' Ark

Noah, the 'comforter,' built an ark at God's behest, and all those outside it died in the flood. God made a covenant with Noah and as a sign, set a seven-hued rainbow in the sky (Gen. 12-14)

Christ's church

Jesus, saviour of the world, founded a church, from which no salvation can be expected, and hence God made a new eternal covenant with the redeemer, whose holy sign are the seven sacraments (John 10,7)

APPENDIX B

From Wiser, Vol 1, item XII, Antichrist, pp. 553, 555, 557

1.   Meaning of the term

By the term 'Antichrist' we generally understand any opponent of the kingdom of mercy and truth founded by Jesus, and in this respect there have always been Antichrists. But in the narrower sense, the term refers to a specific individual, who will appear in the near future and wreak great destruction in the church of God.

4.   On the origins, birth and life of the Antichrist

All the church fathers and writers agree that the origin of the Antichrist is among the Jews. Just as the true Jesus emerged from among them, thus they claim, so the false Jesus came from among them. St. Heronymus comments on the verse in the Book of Daniel: "For he shall come up and shall become strong with a small people (11,23) that the 'small people' is the Jewish people. And thus the holy fathers also believe that the parents of the Antichrist are from the tribe of Dan.

6.   On his kingdom, the wars he wages and his end

It is believed that he is born in Babylon and will extend his reign from there. The Jews will be the first to support him, and he will award them high positions in his kingdom. He will seize treasures of gold and silver. He will conquer Palestine and establish his seat in Jerusalem...

APPENDIX C

From the legend of Andreas from the village Hall of Rin.
In Katholischer Kindergarten, p. 382ff, July 12th

Between the towns of Hall and Insbruck in the Tyrol, stretches a wide and beautiful mountain range. Many pleasant villages and lonely farms are scattered amidst the green mountain scenery. One of the villages is Rin; about fifteen minutes away stands the house where Andreas was born, on November 26, 1459. His father was Simon Oxner and his mother's name was Maria. They were poor but honest peasants. The boys godfather was Hans Maier, of the Weisel farm in Rin. The parents were his tenants. About a year and a half after Andreas was born, his father died, and his mother brought him up alone.

At that time, many traders used to pass along the road near the farm, en route to the great fairs which were held four times a year in the town of Bozen in the southern Tyrol. Among them were many Jews. In 1462, ten Jews travelled this road on their way to the fair which was named after Jesus. As they were passing by the farm, little Andreas, aged two, was sitting and playing outside the door. He was a charming child. When the Jews saw him, they agreed among themselves to kidnap him secretly and kill him out of hatred of Jesus. Had it not been for the mother, who was nearby, they would have taken him on the spot. They went to the nearby tavern, where little Andreas' godfather, Hans Maier, a drunkard, was sitting. The Jews now tried to obtain the child through him.

They conversed with him about different things and asked him about Andreas. Hans told them all he knew, and said that he was the child's guardian and godfather. The Jews praised the child, saying that he deserved a better education than his poor mother could give him; and asked Hans to intercede with the mother to give them the little boy; they would take him with them, be as parents to him, and give him a prosperous and comfortable life. And they promised Hans a hatful of gold coins of he gave them the child.

Miserly Hans, dazzled by the gold, agreed to give them little Andreas when they returned four weeks later from the fair in Bozen.

And thus it came about. The ten Jews, with their teachers or rabbis, returned four weeks later to Kin. It was on July 9th, a Friday, that they returned to the tavern. They asked to spent their Sabbath there. Hans Maier joined them at the bar; he drank a great deal at their expense. They remained there on Sunday as well.

Hans, the godfather, had learned meanwhile that Andreas' mother was leaving early on Monday morning for Ambras to pick vegetables. At this time, he intended to hand over the child to the Jews. Early in the morning, before the mother set out on her journey, she handed the child trustingly and confidently to his godfather and guardian and asked him, with maternal concern, to guard her beloved only child until she returned. The godfather made a false promise.

So the mother went out to the fields to pick vegetables. It was six in the morning. When she had left, and not a soul was nearby, Hans led the Jews through the entrance into the room. There they counted out the promised money into his hat, and he gave them the child. But outside, a great storm began to rage. Lightning flashed, and the thunder was so loud that the entire house shook and the windows rattled. The workers in the fields scattered in all directions, hastening home.

The Jews were very frightened; they feared that the mother would return, so they left the farm and returned to the tavern. There they waited till the storm died down. Then once again they sneaked into the house, where Hans Maier and Andreas had remained. By various promises they persuaded the little boy to go out of the house and with them. They fled into the forest, where the trees and bushes grew thickly. After some time they reached, in the heart of the forest, a large stone protruding from the ground. Its surface was flat but inclined like a crooked table. There they halted. Now the rabbi seized the child and cast him on the stone. They tied his hands behind his back and bound his feet, and, they gagged him with a piece of cloth lest his cries reveal their hiding place.

Now they began to stab and dismember the unhappy child, cursing and vilifying him. They opened his veins and caught his blood; finally they untied his bonds and laid him down, arranging his limbs in the position of a crucifix; then the bloodthirsty rabbi cut his throat. The blood of the sweet and innocent child poured out of his many wounds. These inhuman people did not content themselves with these cruel acts of torture and murder. By the stone stood a birch tree. They took the body and hung it on the tree. And the stone, on which they perpetrated the crime, has been called since then 'The Jew-stone', and can be seen to this day. Then they fled to their lives.

While all this was happening at the Jew-stone in Rin, the mother was in the field. Before the storm began, she felt ill, and suddenly fainted. When the storm died down, she awakened and returned to her work. Suddenly she felt a drop of blood dripping on her right hand; it was still fresh and hot. Maria was startled and showed it to the others; she wiped away the drop with a fearful heart. But immediately afterwards, a second and third drop of fresh blood fell on her hand; the mother wondered at it and was afraid; she felt that it augured ill. Her concern for her child gave her no peace. She rose up, and hastened from Ambras to the farm. She ran to the room first of all to see the cradle where her child lay. But he was not there. In great distress, she sought him throughout the house and then throughout the neighbourhood. Finally she found the godfather, and asked him where he had taken Andreas and where the child was. First, Hans pretended to know nothing. But, because of her cries and sobs, he tried to comfort her and told her to be calm since Andreas was well. He led her to the room and showed her the hat filled with gold. He told her that the masters had promised him that the boy would be given a good education and that they would guarantee his prosperity; he even offered her some of the money. But as he put his hand into the hat, the money turned into dry leaves. Now fate had betrayed the betrayer himself. The mother urged him to reveal where the Jews had gone with her child Hans, now shocked at the divine punishment, admitted everything and admitted that the Jews had taken the child to the forest.

The mother hastened to the forest. She cried out, weeping and calling Andreas' name. She reached the stone, saw the cloth and the bloodstains, and soon discovered the corpse of the little boy hanging on the birch tree. Her heartbreaking cries soon brought people to the spot. They cut down the body and placed it in the arms of the fainting mother. After overcoming her first grief, she arose and went straight to the priest, told him what had happened and discussed the funeral arrangements with him.

Now they carried the sacred corpse to the church in Rin; there he was buried in the courtyard not far from the pulpit.

APPENDIX D

From *Werner*, an epistle from the Royal Consistorium in Koblenz concerning
Jewish education, March 24, 1824, p. 196/7

We too favour a temporary arrangement, since much time will elapse until a general edict is issued. Such an arrangement is vital as so many uneducated Jews go out into the world. Moreover, the harm caused in the Solms-Hohensolmisch district by usury and despicable Jewish petty trade is most aggravatingly evident. It is related that there a certain Jew took over the home of a poor peasant, and offered it up for sale, having gained possession of it for usurious interest for several lengths of cloth.

Since, to the present day, too many of the principles of the Talmud and its commentaries are still inculcated in the old-style Jewish schools, - such as, that the Christian should not be treated as a friend but as an alien - as they call him, 'goy' - and since the tenets of the Talmud permit exploiting the errors of the non-Jew, not restoring lost goods to him, keeping promises only when advantageous, extracting usurious interest from the stranger etc, etc; and since the Talmud describes the most basic and useful tasks of farmers and artisans as unfit for Jews, - therefore, it is necessary to oppose these corrupting principles through proper education in school. Even a temporary arrangement, however imperfect, can serve this important aim...the Jews must regard themselves at this time as obliged more than ever to render their brethren worthy of respect through proper education. If they continue to hold aloof from the general education system, as experience so far has shown, they will be discriminated against as compared to Christians...

APPENDIX E

In *Debus*, complaint of Rabbi Dr. Hollander of Trier, June 1880, p. 296/7

At the request of the Jewish community of Trittenheim, which is affiliated to the Trier rabbinate, I visited there on Sunday, June 13, to inspect religious institutions and to deliver a sermon in the synagogue.

When I arrived in Trittenheim, I found a large part of the local Catholic population assembled by the river bank. With more or less earsplitting yells, this crowd, and particularly the younger people among them, followed me through the village to my destination. Through the window of a small tower by the river, they passed out a stick, to which were tied rags and a bundle of straw. In short, the conduct of the people was such that I was advised to refrain from visiting the synagogue lest I be harmed by the local population. I chose, therefore, to deliver my sermon in a private house.

I was deeply distressed by the uncivilized and intolerant conduct of the people of Trittenheirm, and I appeal to your excellency humbly to denounce this incident and to exert your influence in the proper quarters so that such things will not occur again. Though I cannot attribute responsibility directly to any specific person, I must point out that it is the obligation of those who head the churches and schools of this country to implant in the hearts of both children and adults sincere faith and love for their fellow men, to educate them to be civilized and ethical, and not to pour scorn on people of different faith to their own, when the latter are worshipping their God quietly without causing public disruption...

APPENDIX F

From the proclamation of Catholic policy, 1851, *Bergstrasser*, I, pp. 183/5

Catholic edicts exist everywhere equally, and in Germany as well, according to the following basic tenets:

1. Catholicism sincerely respects liberty and aspires to achieve it, but sees all liberty as bound by the limits of morality. It does not advocate liberty in order to permit the citizen room for arbitrary conduct, but seeks to cooperate with its brethren in a spirit of devotion in order to promote rights and interests which can satisfy the moral demands of the individual and the needs of a community guided by moral principles.

2. Catholicism respects the public order and seeks to maintain it, - not that order imposed on the individual by the police, but that which will constitute the basis for a constitutional human society conducting itself according to the divine ideal.

3. Catholicism respects the organic development shaping collective life.

4. Catholicism seeks sincerely to promote the public welfare...

NOTES ON THE APPENDICES

These six appendices were selected in order to demonstrate the nature of the Catholic arguments against the Jews in Germany. The order in which they have been cited is intended to indicate a certain development in these anti-Jewish claims. The first appendix illustrates the theory that the Jewish Scriptures as the harbinger of the Christian message. It quotes the Church Fathers, (see the first part of the document, not quoted here: "As general signs, the church fathers refer us to Adam (*Ibid.*, p. 125). The biblical exegesis was generally accepted by the architects of Christian tenets of faith, and hence, the text quoted here was not an aberration. In accordance with the Christian outlook, Christian theology attempts to show , through textual evidence, the inferior nature of the Old Testament. It is not judged on its own merits, but in light of its function of paving the way for the New Testament. The comparisons are intended to lend a historical dimension to the appearance of Jesus. The parallel between Moses, who liberated the people from slavery, and Jesus, freeing them from servitude to Satan, is particularly forced. Satan is still referred to neutrally, and it is clear that the reference is to any denier of Christianity, viz. Appendix B, in the definition of "Antichrist" as 'a specific individual, who will appear in the near future and wreak great destruction in the church of God".

The "Satan-Antichrist" identification is not necessarily implied by the Church Fathers, but was seized upon by the preachers. They were able to rest their case on the hypothesis of the church fathers that the Antichrist was of Jewish origin, as stated in Appendix B. Christian theology acknowledged two kingdoms on earth. One was that of Christ, the other- of Satan, all mortals being divided between the two.[1] Hence the Jewish Antichrist, who denies the kingdom of Christ, belongs to the kingdom of Satan.

We have included in the appendixes the Rin blood-libel, and it should be stated at once that the intention was not to describe the event as an example of this type of defamation. "The church did not officially accept this charge as true, and the popes tried to combat this false charge."[2] Of trials based on blood libels in the period before the First World War, Flusser

152

stated that the motives were ulterior ones extraneous to the church. The
story we quote can help elucidate two issues relevant to our discussion:

First, the fact that the story was printed and disseminated as a book of
Kindergarten stories indicates how the negative and barbaric image of the
Jew was inculcated in wide sections of the German people. This is a classic
example of education in anti-semitism, sponsored and recommended by a
Catholic bishop, for Kindergarten children. The book's popularity is
demonstrated by its circulation. The seventh edition appeared in 1911, and
the first four editions reached thirteen thousand copies each. The book was
also translated into many European languages. According to the foreword,
which served as a testimonial from the church: "These are selected excerpts
which can enhance the weak understanding of children and warm their
hearts...This book carefully omits anything which might harm the tender
conscience and the innocent heart."[3] When such stories are used for
educational purposes - and there are other similar stories in the book - the
image created is so repulsive and cruel that the Jew is seen as truly
subhuman. Thus the foundation was prepared on which the Nazis could
some day build, claiming that they were serving the Christian cause.

The second point relates to the independence and standing of the
minor clergy, on the one hand and Catholic publicistic writing, on the other.
One might have expected such false arguments to have been abandoned, in
light of the papal reservations. However, popular hatred and simplification
prevailed over theological attitudes imposed from above. And, as has been
claimed in this book, the confrontation between Jews and Catholics (as well
as Protestants) took place in the everyday sphere, which contributed to the
prevailing mood. A Catholic newspaper referred to the "popular fury"
aroused as a consequence of rumours of blood-libels. It was said there: "It
must be admitted that the popular imagination has often unjustly accused the
Jews of murdering children, but, on the other hand, it cannot be denied that
the murder of children for ritual purposes did in fact take place....The fact
that the truth of these weighty charges could not always be proved in courts
of law should not surprise us, because of the influence which the Alliance
Israelite exerted through gold."[4]

This statement reflects a simple refusal to forgo the advantages which could be derived from disseminating these horror tales about Jews. One should not seek consistency in these stories since, as is the case with other manifestations of anti-semitism, the criteria of factual truth are irrelevant here. Thus, it was possible for someone to write that he did not believe that medieval Jews poisoned wells, and that Jewish physicians murdered their Christian patients, but where the murder of Christian children was concerned "I am totally convinced that in the Middle Ages this charge was justified, and that in Germany this justification is still valid...Murder for ritual purposes in the Germany of today is no legend...It transpires from the Jewish adherence to ancient traditions (see descriptions of the Alliance Israelite in 1890 concerning the Jews of Tripoli: superstition and adherence to ancient customs are dangerous). And, again, the Mosaic religion is a tribal religion which regards all non-Jewish humans and animals as mere objects..."[5]

It seems that the accusation of ritual murder as a religious crime was not the focal point of the attacks on Jews. It was revived in order to reinforce the image of the corrupt Jew, bribing his surroundings with gold and denying the humanity of the Christian. The two above quotations, which differ in essence, both mention the Alliance Israelite. This too is indicative of a trend to highlight the international character of Jewish power. This argument was popular among antisemites.

The extent to which the negative image was absorbed by the population is shown in the two last appendixes. The distortion and falsification in descriptions of the Talmud and its influence recall the diatribes against the Talmud in the nineteenth century. The Catholic sees himself as under attack for his Christianity: it is rejected by the Jew, because of the "corrupting principles" of the Talmud.

The behaviour of the Trittenheim population towards the rabbi attests to the atmosphere among the Christian villagers vis a vis the Jews. It indicates their contempt for all Jews.

The five documents quoted here reflect the sequence which has been discussed in this book: the transition from the theological dictate to popular vulgarization, from denigration of the Jewish Scriptures to contempt for the Jewish character.

The sixth document deals with Catholic political organization in Germany. As the Catholics became an organized socio-political force, they sought increasingly to exert influence on wider sectors of the German population. Their open dissociation from anti-semitism did not mitigate their rejection of the Jews, as documented in this book. This fact explains the consensus on the Jewish question, which prevailed in most Catholic circles, before and after the political organization, and both above and below the surface.

NOTES

1.   Trachtenberg, p. 41.

2.   Flusser, Motza Alilot, p. 19. (Hebrew)

3.   Data cited in Lehr, pp. 176, 178. Even today, these stories sometimes resurface. The story of Andreas of Rin was republished in 1947; see on this Eckert, p. 306.

4.   Wahrheit, Vol. 4, Munich 1898, pp. 264, 265.

5.   Boenigk, pp. 144, 146.

NAMES MARKED IN TEXT WITH AN ASTERISK

1. *Bea, Augustin (1881-1968).*
    Cardinal, Catholic theologian, Jesuit, professor of biblical studies in Holland. Appointed by the Pope Chief Secretary at the Office for Christian Unification. Very active at the Second Vatican Synod for rapprochement between Jews and Christians and between Catholic and non-Catholic Christians.

2. *Bertram, Adolph Johannes (1859- 1945).*
    From 1919 onwards, served as Chairman of the Bishops Conference at Fulda. Known for his opposition to the Nazi regime.

3. *Collingwood, Robin (1889-1943).*
    British philosopher and archaeologist, Professor at Oxford.

4. *Doellinger, Joh. Joseph Ignaz (1799-1890).*
    Priest Professor of the History of Ecclesiastical Law at Eschfenberg and Munich. Was active with Goerres in the founding of the Historisch-Politischen Blaetter, and fought for the independence of the Catholic Church. Delegate to the National Assembly in Frankfurt in 1840-1848, opposed the declaration of papal infallibility, and was excommunicated by the Pope in 1871 as a consequence. Was the focus of the Altkatolikan church, which sought to free itself of dependence n the Vatican.

5. *Faulhaber, Michael von (1869-1952).*
    Archbishop of Munich. Professor of Biblical Studies. Cardinal. Took a courageous stand against the Nazi regime and struggle for church independence and for human rights.

6.   *Goerres, Joseph (1776-1848).*

Essayist, philosopher. Supporter of the French Revolution and the establishment of a republic in the Thine region. Publisher of the Reinische Merkur, where he attacked Napoleon. From 1827, Professor of History at Munich University, where he was the center of a circle of Catholics who supported the establishment of a 'greater Germany' with Austria. In 1838, he founded the Historisch-Politischen Blaetter.

7.   *Jarke, Carl Ernst (1801-1852).*

Essayist and jurist. One of the founders of the Historische Blaetter. Fought for the independence of the Catholic church from the secular establishment.

8.   *Ketteler, Wilhelm Emanuel, Freiherr von (1811-1877).*

Bishop of Mainz, jurist. Delegate to the National Assembly of Frankfurt. Among the fighters for the Catholic cause during the Kulturkampf. Pioneer of social policies on behalf of Catholic workers.

9.   *Meiser, Hans (1881-1956).*

German evangelical theologian. 1933-1955 - Bishop of the Evangelical-Lutheran church in Bavaria. Under the Nazis, active in the Bekennde Kirche (Confessing Church).

10.   *H. Mueller, Adam (1779-1829).*

Theoretician of social and political science. In 1805 converted from Protestantism to Catholicism, opposed the ideals of the Emancipation and Adam Smith's liberal theories. Organized opposition to Hardenberg's reforms.

11.   *Reichensperger, August (1808-1895).*

One of the prominent figures in the Catholic Center Party. One of the main opponents of Bismarck's anti-Catholic policies.

12.   *Sombart Werner (1863-1941).*
Economist and sociologist. Professor in Breslau and Berlin. Expert on the economic development of the transition from capitalism to socialism. Known for the anti-semitic theories in his books.

13.   *Weiss, Albert Maria (1844-1925).*
Writer and sociologist. Author of the 'Apologie', a five-volume work in defence of the Christian church.

14.   *Windthorst, Ludwig (1812-1891).*
Most important leader of political Catholicism in Germany. After 1871, leader of the Catholic Center Party. One of Bismarck's fiercest opponents because of the latter's anti-Catholic policies in the era of the Kulturkampf.

15.   *Wurm, Theophil (1868-1953).*
Evangelical theologian. From 1933 Bishop of Wurtemburg. Among the central spokesmen against Nazi interference in church affairs.

SERMONS AND CATHOLIC LITERATURE - PRIMARY SOURCES

Abbt, Benedikt

Katholische Geheimnissreden, Augsburg, 1885.

Colmar, Joseph Ludwig

Predigten, Hrg. von Freunden und Verehrern des Verewigten, Mainz, 1859.

Das Zweite Vatikanische Konzil, Freiburg, 1964 Bde. I-III.

Deharbe, Joseph/1

Gruendliche und leichtfassliche Erklaerung des Katholizismus, Hilfsbuch fuer den Katechetischen Unterricht in der Schule und in der Kirche. Paderborn, 1872.

Deharbe, Joseph/2

Populaeres Lehrbuch der Religion oder der Katholische Katechismus. Ein Lesebuch fuer Christliche Familien und ein Handbuch fuer Katecheten Muenster, 1851.

Der Praktische Katechet in Kirche und Schule Eine Sammlung Vollstaendig Ausgearbeiteter Katechesen Nach Dem Katholischen Katechismus Wuerzburg, 1879.

Diessel, Gerhard

Predigten und Konferenzen, Paderborn 1913.

Dreher, Bruno

Biblische Predigten. Ein Homiletisches Werkbuch, Stuttgart, 1968.

Ehrler, Joseph

Apologethische Predigten, 1877.

Endler, Franz

Apologethische Vortraege ueber die Gottheit Jesu fuer die Gebildeten aller Staende.

Frank, Karl	*Weide meine Laemmer. Die Heilige Geschichte der Jugend erzaehlt und erklaert in Kinderpredigten,* Halle 1897. *zunaechst aber fuer Studierende,* Prag, 1900.
Frommel, Max	*Pilgerpostille. Predigten fuer das ganze Kirchenjahr nach freien Texten,* Bremen, 1890.
Fuhlrott, Joseph	*Neue Predigten auf alle Sonn -und Festtage des Kirchenjahres,* Regensburg, 1886.
Gradaus, Hiob	*Verschaemte Predigten. Schwarzbrod fuer's Christenvolk,* Regensburg, 1862.
Hammerstein, L.v	*Begruendung des Glaubens,* Trier, 1900.
Heim, Franz Anton	*Predigt-Magazin. In Verbindung mit mehreren Katholischen Gelehrten, Predigern und Seelsorgern,* Augsburg, 1839.
Heinz-Mohr, Gerhard	*Die Sau mit dem goldenen Haarband. Herzhafte Predigten aus alter und neuer Zeit.* Duesseldorf Koeln, 1973.
Huller, Georg	*Ausgewaehlte Volkspredigten auf Sonntage und Feste des Katholischen Kirchenjahres,* Augsburg 1871.
Hungari, Anton	*Musterpredigten der Katholischen Kanzel-Beredsamkeit Deutschlands aus der neueren und neuesten Zeit,* Mainz, 1859.
Katholik	*Der Katholik. Eine Religioese Zeitschrift zur Belehrung und Warnung, 1821-1859.*
Katholischer	
Kindergarten	*oder Legende fuer Kinder,* 4. Aufl. Freib. 1889.
Kirchliches Handlexidon	*In Verbindung mit einer Anzahl Ev. Lutherischer Theologen Herausgegeben* Leipzig, 1891.

Klerusblatt	*Organ der Diozesen-Priestervereine Bayerns.*
Koerber, J.	*Predigten fuer die Sonntage und Hauptfeste des Herrn. Nach den Episteln und Evangelien des Kirchenjahres,* Muenchen, 1898.
Kotte, Anton	*Die Heilige Mission oder Ausfuehrliche Erwaegungen Jener Heilswahrheiten Welch Bei Den Missionen Vorgetragen werden,* Regensburg, 1857.
Kroenes, Franz Edmund	*Homiletisches Real-Lexikon,* Regensburg, 1860.
	Homiletischer Wegweiser durch das ganze Katholische Kirchenjahr mittelst einer vollstaendigen Uebersicht und Einteilung des Inhalts aller Sonn -und Festtaetigen Episteln und Evangelien, Regensburg, 1862.
Kuhn, Johannes	*Katholische Dogmatik,* Tuebingen, 1859.
Lettan, H	*Biblische Geschichte fuer Schulen,* Leipzig, 1901.
Lexikon, Auflage	*Lexikon fuer Theologie und Kirche,* Zweite Begruendet von M. Buchberger, Hrsg. von J. Hoefer und K. Rahner, Freiburg, 1957.
Lierheimer, Xav.Fr.	*Jesus fuer uns. Predigten Heilige Messopfer,* 1872.
Martin, Konrad	*Christenthum und Papstthum. Hirtenwort an meine Dioecesanen.* Paderborn, 1867.
Mauch, Andreas	*Die Kirchliche und Politische Freiheit in ihrer Bedeutung fuer Einander und fuer die Gesell schaft. Zwei Predigten mit Ruecksicht auf die Bewegungen der Zeit,* Stuttgart, 1848.
Mehler, Ludwig	*Ein Handbuch fuer Religionslehrer, Katecheten und Prediger. Zugleich Handbuch zur belehrenden und erbauenden Lektuere fuer Christliche Familien,* Regensburg, 1894.

164

Melchers, Paulus	*Die Katholische Lehre von der Kirche* Koeln, 1881.
Nickel, Joseph	*Predigten auf die Sonntage und Feste des Kirchenjahres,* 1854.
Patiss, Georg	*Kurze Homelien ueber die Sonntags Evangelien des Kirchenjahres fuer das glaeubige Volk,* Innsbruck, 1882.
Paulhuber	*Reden ueber die Christ-Katholische Religionslehre im Allgemeinen,* Regensburg, 1849.
Philothea	*Blaetter fuer religioese Belehrung und Erbauung durch Predigten.* Wuerzburg.
Rolfus	*Die Glubens und Sittenlehre der Katholischen Kirche. Ein Hand und Hausbuch fuer Katecheten und Christliche Familien,* Koeln, 1874.
Saffenreuther, Georg J	*Predigten,* Wuerzburg, 1840.
Scherer, P.A.	*Bibliothek fuer Prediger,* 1888.
Schmitt, Jakob	*Erklaerung des mittleren Deharbeschen Katechismus zunaechst fuer die mittlere und hoehere Klasse der Elementarschulen,* Freiburg, 1889.
Schmuelling, Th	*Predigten fuer die Advents und Weihnachtszeit,* Muenster, 1882.
Segur, Abbe De	*Kurze und einfache Antworten auf die meist verbreiteten Einwendungen gegen die Religion Mit Antworten auf mehr besonders in Deutschland gangbare Einwendungen gengen die Kirche,* Osnabrueck, 1852.
Siebert, Anton	*Geistlicher Sturmbock oder Kapuziner-Predigten fuer Stadt und Land zur Bekehrung oder zum Davonlaufen,* Regensburg, 1856.
Ventura, Joachim P.	*Die Christliche Politik, Conferenzen,* aus dem Franzoesischen von Ph. Kuelb, Mainz, 1858.

Weiss, Albert Maria

Apologie des Christenthums vom Standpunkte der Sitte und Kultur, Freiburg, 1888.

Wenzel, Joseph P.

Vortraege fuer studierende Jugend, Mainz, 1880.

Wetzer and Welte's

Kirchenlexikon. Encyklopaedie der Katholischen Theologie und ihre Hilfswissenschaften, Freiburg, 1889.

Wiser, Thomas

Vollstaendiges Lexikon fuer Prediger und Katecheten in welchem die Katholischen Glauben und Sittenlehren ausfuehrlich betrachtet sind Bd. 1-16, Regensburg, 1862-1863.

Wolfgarten, Gottfried

Ganz Kurze Fruehreden fuer drei Jahrgaenge Mainz, 1891.

Zollner, Ev. Johann

Das Katholische Christenthum, seine Heiligen Handlungen, Zeiten und Orten, Predigten ueber die Gesammt-Lithurgie der Katholischen Kirche Regensburg, 1869.

BIBLIOGRAPHY OF QUOTED LITERATURE

Alexander, Edgar

Church and Society in Germany. Social and Political Movements and Ideas in German and Austrian Catholicism, 1789-1950, N.Y., 1953.

Almog, Samuel (Ed.)

Sinat Yisrael Ledorotea, Jerusalem, 1990 (Hebrew).

Arndt, Ino

Die Judenfrage im Licht der evangelischen Sonntagsblaetter von 1918-1933, Diss. 1960 Tuebingen (Unveroeffentlicht).

Bacharach, Zwi

Racism-The Tool of Politics. From Monism Towards Nazism. Jerusalem 1985 (Hebrew)

Modern Antisemitism, Tel-Aviv 1979 (Hebrew).

Ideologies in the Twentieth Century, Tel-Aviv, 1980 (Hebrew).

Man in the Nazi Conception, in: *Massuah, A Yearbook on the Holocaust and Heroism*, Tel-Aviv 1986 (Hebrew).

Bachem, Karl

Vorgeschichte, Geschichte und Politik der Deutschen Zentrumspartei, 1815-1914 Koeln, 1927.

Baeck, Leo (Institut)

Juden im Wilhelminischen Deutschland, 1890-1914, Schriftenreihe Wissenschaftlicher Abhandlungen des LBI. Bd.33, Tuebingen, 1976.

Bauer, Bruno

Die Judenfrage, Braunschewig, 1843.

Bein, Alexander

Haparasit Hayehudi, Yalkut Moreshet, 1966 (Hebrew).

Bergstraesser

Politischer Katholizismus. Dokumente seiner Entwickelung, Muenchen,

168

Guetersloh, 1921/3. Bd., I, II, Hildesheim, N.Y., 1976.

Bishop, Clair Huchet

How Catholics look at Jews. Inquiries into Italian, Spanish and French Teaching Materials. N.Y., Toronto, 1974.

Bloch, Joseph

Israel und die Voelker nach Juedischer Lehre, Berlin, Wien, 1922.

Boenigk, Otto Frh.von

Grundzuege zur Judenfrage. Soziologisch-oekonomische Studie, Leipzig, 1894.

Bracher, Karl D.

Die Deutsche Diktatur, Entstehung, Struktur Folgen des National-Sozialismus, Berlin 1969.

Cohn, Haim H.

Supreme Court Judge-Talks with Michael Shashar, Jerusalem 1989 (Hebrew).

Cohn, N.

Warrant for Genocide, Tel Aviv 1967 (Hebrew).

Collingwood, R.G.

The Idea of History, Oxford, (1943) 1963.

Christlich-Soziale Blaetter

Katholisches Sozial-Central Organ. 1868-1898.

Debus, Karl Heinz

Dokumentation zur Geschichte der Juedischen Bevoelkerung im Rheinland-Pfalz und im Saarland von 1800-1945. Bd.4, Koblenz, 1974.

Denzler, Georg
Fabricius, Volker

Die Kirchen im Dritten Reich. Christen und Nazis Hand in Hand? Bd. 1,2, Frankfurta/M 1984.

Die Wahrheit

(Hrg) Wasserburg, Philip, Muenchen Bd.5, 1899.

Der Mauscheljude

Von einem Deutschen Advokaten fuer Deutsche Christen aller Bekenntnisse, Paderborn, 1880.

Eckert, W.P. & Ehrlich, E.L.

Judenhass-Schuld der Christen? Versuch eines Gespraeches, Essen, 1964.

Eschelbacher, Joseph	*Das Judentum und das Wesen des Christen tums. Vergleichende Studien*, Berlin, 1908.
Ettinger, Shumel	*Modern Anti-Semitism, Studies and Essays*, Tel-Aviv 1978 (Hebrew).
Flannery, Edward G.	*The Anquish Of The Jews, Twenty-Three Centuries Of Anti-semitism.* Toronto, 1975.
Flusser, David	*Jewish Sources in Early Christianity. Studies and Essays.* Tel-Aviv 1979 (Hebrew).
	Jesus in Selbstzeugnissen und Bilddokumenten Humburg, 1968.
	Moza Alilot Hadam, in: *Mischpatim We Alilot-Dam*, Tel Aviv, 1967 (Hebrew).
Ginzel, Geunther	*Auschwitz als Herausforderung fuer Juden und Christen*, Heidelberg, 1980.
Greive, Hermann	*Geschichte des modernen Antisemitismus in Deutschland*, Darmstadt, 1983.
	Theologie und Ideologie, Katholozismus und Judentum in Deutschland und Oesterreich, 1918-1935 Heidelberg, 1969.
Guttmann, Michael	*Das Judentum und seine Umwelt. Eine Darstellung der religioesen und rechtlichen Beziehungen zwischen Juden und nicht-Juden mit besonderer Beruecksichtigung der Talmudisch-Rabbinischen Quellen*, Berlin, 1927.
Haase, Amine	*Katholische Presse und die Judenfrage. Inhalts analyse. Katholischer Periodika am Ende des 19 Jahrhunderts.* Pullach bei Muenchen, 1975.
Hay, Malcom	*The Foot of Pride. The Pressure of Christendom on the People of Israel for 1900 Years.* Boston, 1950.
Historische-Politiche Blaetter	*fuer das Katholische Deutschland, 1838-1923.*

Herr, Friedrich

Gottes Erste Liebe. Die Juden im Spannungsfeld der Geschichte, (1967), Muenchen, 1986.

Herder

Herders Conversations-Lexikon, 1854.

Hertz, Frederick

The German Public Mind in the Nineteenth Century, London, 1975.

Hilberg, Raul

The Destruction Of The European Jews, (1960), Chicago, 1967.

Historikerstreit

Die Dokumentation der Kontroverse um die Einzigartigkeit der nationalsozialistischen Judenvernichtung Muenchen, Zuerich, 1987.

Hitler, Adolf

Mein Kampf, 10. Auflage, 1942.

Hochland

Monatsschrift fuer alle Gebiete des Wissens, der Literatur und Kunst. Muth, Karl (Hrg).

Hoess, Rudolf

Kommandant in Auschwitz. Autobiographische Aufzeichnungen des Rudolf Hoess. (Hrg) Martin Broszat (1963) Muenchen 1978.

Hollstein, Dorothea

Jud Suess und die Deutschen, Antisemitische Vorurteile im Nationalsozialistischen Spiefilm, Frankfurt a/M, 1983.

Isaac, Jules

Jesus et Israel, Paris, 1948.

Jaeckel, Eberhard

Hitlers Weltanschauung. Entwurf einer Herrschaft, Tuebingen, 1969.

Hitlers saemtliche Aufzeichnungen, 1905-1924 Stuttgart, 1980.

Jochmann, Werner

Adolf Hitler. Monologe im Fuehrer-Hauptquartier 1941-1944. Die Aufzeichnungen Heinrich Heims, Hamburg 1980.

Gesellschaftskrise und Judenfeindschaft in Deutschland 1870-1945, Hamburg, 1988.

Katz, Jacob	*From Prejudice to Destruction: Antisemitism 1700-1933.* Cambridge, Mass. 1980.
	Out of the Getto. The Social Background of Jewish Emancipation 1770-1870, New York, 1978.
	Die Historische Bedeutung der Judenemanzipation. In: *Zur Assimilation und Emanzipation der Juden,* Darmstadt, 1982.
Ketteler, Wilhelm Emmanuel Fr.von	*Schriften, Aufsaetze und Reden,* Mainz, 1977.
Kirchenblatt	*Westfaelisches Kirchenblatt fuer Katholiken* 20 Jhrg. 1867.
Klein, Charlotte	*Theologie und Anti-Juaismus,* Muenchen, 1975.
Kulka, Otto D. Mendes-Flohr, Paul R.	*Judaism and Christainity under the Impact of National Socialism,* Jerusalem, 1987.
Lagarde, Paul De	*Ausgewaehlte Schriften,* Muenchen, 1924.
Lehr, Stefan	*Antisemitismus-Religioese Motive im sozialen Vorurteil,* Muenchen, 1974.
Leibowitz, Yeshayahu	*Notes to the Weekly Tora Readings,* Jerusalem, 1988.
Lewy, Guenter	*The Catholic Church and Nazi Germany,* N.Y. 1964.
Liefmann, E.	Antichrist und Ahasverus, in: *Judaica, Beitraege zum Verstaendnis des Juedischen Schicksals in Vergangenheit und Gegenwart,* 3, Zuerich, 1947.
Lohalm, Uwe	*Voelkischer Radikalismus. Die Geschichte des Deutschvoelkischen Schutz-und Trutz-Bundes 1919-1923,* Hamburg, 1970.
Marr, Wilhelm	*Der Sieg des Judenthums ueber das Germanenthum*

172

	Vom Nicht-Confessionalen Standpunkt aus betrachtet, Bern, 1879.
Massing, Paul	*Vorgeschichte des Politischen Antisemitismus* Frankfurt a/M, 1959.
Moody, Joseph N.	*Church and Society, Catholic Social and Political Thought and Movements 1789-1950.* N.Y., 1953.
Moore, G.F.	Christian Writers on Judaism, *Harvard Theological Review* XIV, no. 3, July 1921, pp. 197-254.
Mosse, George	*Germans and Jews*, N.Y., 1971.
	The Crisis Of German Ideology, Intellectual Origins Of The Third Reich, N.Y., 1964.
Mueller, Hans	*Katholische Kirche und Nationalsozialismus* Muenchen, 1965.
Neubaur, L.	*Die Sage vom Ewigen Juden*, Leipzig, 1864.
	Neue Mitteilungen ueber die Sage vom Ewigen Juden, Leipzig, 1893.
New Catholic	*Encyclopedia, The Catholic University of,* Washington, D.C., 1981.
Nietsche, F.	*Jenseits von Gut und Boese*, 1887.
Niewyk, Donald L.	*The Jews in Weimar Germany*, Louisiana State University Press, 1980.
Oberman, Heiko A.	*The Roots of Antisemitism In the Age of Renaissance and Reformation*, Philadelphia, 1984.
Olmesdahl, Ruth	*Die Juden und der Tod Jesu. Anti-juedische Motive in den evangelischen Reiligions buechern fuer die Grundschule*, Neukirchen Vluyn, 1981.
Organ	*fuer den Windthorstbund*, 1898.
Parkes, James	*The Jew in Medieval Community*, N.Y., 1976.

	The Conflict of the Church and the Synagogue, Cleveland & New York, 1961.
	Antisemitism, London, 1963.
Pfisterer, Rudolf	*Von A- bis Z. Quellen zu Fragen um Juden und Christen*, Wuppertal-Barmen, 1971.
Pulzer, Peter	*The Rise of Political Anti-Semitism in Germany and Austria*, New-York, London, 1964.
Rauschning, Hermann	*Hitler Speaks*, London, 1940.
Rengstorf, H.von Kortzfleisch, S.v	*Kirche und Synagoge, Handbuch zur Geschichte von Christen und Juden. Darstellung mit Quellen.* Stuttgart, 1970.
Renan, Ernest	*Histoire Générale Et Système Comparée des Lanques Semetiques*. Paris, MDCCC.
Richarz, Monika A	*Juedisches Leben in Deutschland. Zur Sozial-geschichte., 1780-1871*, Stuttgart, 1976.
B	*Juedisches Leben in Deutschland. Zeugnisse zur Sozialgeschichte im Kaiserreich, 1871-1914*, Stuttgart, 1979.
Rosenzweig, F.	*Der Stern Der Erloesung*, Jerusalem, 1970 (Hebrew Ed.).
Ruerup, Reinhard	Emanzipation und Antisemitismus. Historische Verbindungen. In: H. Strauss & N. Kampe. (Hrsg *Antisemitismus, Von der Judenfeindschaft zum Holocaust,* Frankfurt, N.Y., 1985.
Rundbrief	*Freiburger Rundbrief, Beitraege zur Christlich-Juedischen Begegnung.*
Sartre, Jean P.	*Réflexions sur la Question Juive,* Paris 1946.
Schemann, Ludwig	*Die Rasse in Geisteswissenschaften,* Muenchen 1928, S. 385.

174

Schnabel, Franz

Deutsche Geschichte im 19. Jahrhundert. Bd. 4 Die Religioesen Kraefte, Freiburg, 1951.

Schoeps, Hans Joachim

Juedisch-Christliches Religionsgesparaech in neunzehn Jahrhunderten. Geschichte einer Theologischen Auseinandersetzung, Berlin, 1937.

Scholder, Klaus

Die Kirchen und das Dritte Reich Frankfurt, Berlin (1977) 1986.

Schramm, Gottfried

Die Juden als Minderheit in der Geschichte . Versuch eines Resumees. Muenchen, 1981.

Sombart, Werner

The Jews and Modern Capitalism, N.Y. 1962.

Sontheimer, Kurt

Antidemokratisches Denken in der Weimarer Republik (1962) Muenchen, 1978.

Staatslexikon

Im Auftrag der Goerres-Gesellschaft unter Mitwirkung zahlreicher Fachleute Fuenfte Auflage, Freiburg/B, 1927.

Stahl, Julius F.

Der Christliche Staat und sein Verhaeltnis zum Deismus und Judenthum. Eine durch die Verhandlungen des Vereinigten Landtags her vorgerufene Abhandlung, Berlin, 1847.

Sterling, Eleonore

Er ist wie Du. Aus der Fruehgeschichte des Antisemitismus in Deutschland, Muenchen, 1956.

Stern, Fritz

The Politics Of Cultural Despair. A Study In The Rise Of The German Ideology, New York, (1961) 1965.

Tal, U.

Christians and Jews in the "Second Reich" (1870-1914), Jerusalem, 1985 (Hebrew ed.).

Patterns in the Contemporary Jewish-Christian Dialogue, Jerusalem, 1969.

Talmon, J.L.

The Age of Violence, Tel-Aviv, 1974 (Hebrew).

182

Y

Yahil, Leni, 14-n11

Z

Zohar, 118
Zollner, Ev. Johann, 33-n16, 43-
n13, 61-n14